I0485675

CHARTING JAMAICA'S ECONOMIC AND SOCIAL DEVELOPMENT
- A much needed paradigm shift

By Dennis Chung FCA, MSc

Foreword by the Honourable Dennis Lalor, OJ

Author's contacts:
E-mail   : dra_chung@hotmail.com
Blog   : dcjottings.blogspot.com

Printed in the USA   ISBN: 978-1441461407

Dedicated to my son, Dennis Chung Jr, and the children of Jamaica

My dream is to one day see a Jamaica where (i) political views are not divisive; (ii) all citizens can feel safe at anytime and anywhere in Jamaica to go about their lawful and productive business; (iii) every Jamaican has the opportunity to maximize their education and life potential; (iv) Jamaica's, and across the globe, supermarkets and stores are filled with products branded "Made in Jamaica"; and (v) the name Jamaica symbolizes pride in everything it is associated with, not just sports or music.

Contents

Tables

Charts

ACKNOWLEDGMENTS

The author wishes to acknowledge the contribution of those who have assisted by reviewing this publication in a very short time. The contribution proved invaluable in the final production.

I would also like to thank the Honourable Dennis Lalor for his encouragement, after long hours of discussion, and contribution by way of kindly consenting to write the foreword for this publication.

My inspiration for writing this came from the people of Jamaica who have never given up no matter how hard the struggles are. They have repeatedly proven their resilience having gone through the unstable period of the 1970s, the structural adjustment of the 1980s, the crisis of the 1990s, and the economic stagnation of the 2000s.

My hope is that Jamaica will pursue this much needed paradigm shift to secure the future of its children.

Dennis Chung FCA, M.Sc.
January 2009

GLOSSARY

BITU	- Bustamante Industrial Trade Union	MOU	- Memorandum of Understanding
BOJ	- Bank of Jamaica	NWU	- National Workers' Union
C/A	- Current Account	OECD	- Organization for Economic Co-operation and Development
EU	- European Union		
EUROSTAT	- Statistical Office of the European Communities	PIOJ	- Planning Institute of Jamaica
FDI	- Foreign Direct Investments	PNP	- People's National Party
FINSAC	- Financial Sector Adjustment Company	PSOJ	- Private Sector Organization of Jamaica
GDP	- Gross Domestic Product	STATIN	- Statistical Institute of Jamaica
IMF	- International Monetary Fund	UNCTAD	- United Nations Development Programme
JHTA	- Jamaica Hotel and Tourist Association	UNDP	- United Nations Development Programme
JLP	- Jamaica Labour Party	UWI	- University of the West Indies
KSAC	- Kingston and St. Andrew Corporation	WER	- IMF World Economic Report
MOFP	- Ministry of Finance and Planning	WIR	- World Investment Report

F o r e w o r d

Written by the Honourable Dennis Lalor, O.J.

If nothing else, "Charting Jamaica's Economic and Social Development" has introduced a new word to the lexicon, "Accountonomics", upon which author Dennis Chung is relying on offering proposals for achieving economic and social development. But the publication goes much further, for throughout its pages Chung shares in detail his views on what is wrong with Jamaica and proposes approaches to tackle them.

The author, as he reveals throughout, underpins his beliefs in the development of a management response through hardnosed strategic planning but he goes beyond these things in his desire to help us to be better prepared to make our country a more worthy place.

From literacy through to the structure and modalities of Government, Chung's passion is revealed, and never more is this displayed than in respect of the political process by which we have been governed since Jamaica's independence in 1962. For while recognizing the need to have the country's economy properly structured to achieve sustainable real quality growth, he argues that before any significant and sustainable progress can be made, Jamaica must first define and implement a new political and social order suited to its size and cultural practices.

He laments the country's failure to capitalize on the economic and social development of the high level growth period of the 1960's due, he argues, to the social and political changes occurring during the 1970's which "set the pace for the country's continued struggle to achieve". And he blames Government policies for the inefficient allocation of resources and the copying of other countries, which we are not necessarily alike, for our failure to focus on areas in which there is a comparative advantage.

On the matter of the much talked about country's debt/GDP ratio, Chung's view is that "debt is good" as long as the marginal return from each dollar of debt is greater than the marginal cost. The role of debt, he feels should be to generate real economic growth, not just in terms of constant prices, but also as it relates to the contribution to the economy. The challenge he states is how to channel debt to a greater level of productivity.

1

In "Charting Jamaica's Economic & Social Development", the author makes it clear that Jamaica must find a way to ensure that Government policies are aligned with the objective of economic and social development and that the global financial crisis (2007/08) has presented the opportunity to examine and decide on the best model for development.

It is a mark of Dennis Chung's own sense of civic responsibility that he has now made his thoughts available to wider audiences than those addressed in his speeches and published articles.

In this he has done the state a service.

Honourable Dennis Lalor, OJ
January 2009

Introduction

I.   **Defining a need**: Since the high levels of economic growth during the 1960s Jamaica has failed to achieve any sustained period of growth. In fact over the 36 years between 1972 and 2007 Jamaica's growth has averaged only around two percent per annum. What is even more important is that Jamaica has failed to achieve relative economic and social development, even during the 1960s high growth period. A review of the GDP growth numbers over the years could support the position that Jamaica was on the way to economic and social development but that the intervening social and political changes of the 1970s lay the foundation for Jamaica's continued struggle to achieve development that kept pace with similar countries. This argument has been posited by many; with others saying that the social changes were necessary. Whatever the outcome of this continuing discussion, one thing is certain, and that is that the period of the 1970s saw significant declines in GDP following on the record growth levels of the 1960s.

There is no arguing that in absolute terms Jamaica has seen some form of development, especially on a social level, but when compared to the economic development of similar countries[1], especially within CARICOM, Jamaica has fallen short.

Many Jamaicans have never known what it is like to understand the meaning of hope in Jamaica, as captured in the quote below.

"Like maybe about three or four generations of Jamaicans, I was born after independence and grew up in Jamaica during the 1970s to 1990s. So excuse my cynicism and urgency for a better Jamaica. I have never known what it is like to be in a Jamaica that is prosperous

---

[1] Measured in real GDP growth percentages

and is looking towards a brighter future. So while you all reminisce about the hope in 1962 and the good times of the 1960s, remember that all I know about Jamaica is the state of emergency in the 1970s, the 1980 election, the black market and foreign exchange restrictions in the 1980s, the financial crisis and high crime rate of the 1990s, and the anaemic growth and fiscal deficits continuing into the new century of the 2000s."[2]

This is a message shared by many Jamaicans who have often wondered why we are unable to get out of this downward spiral of economic and social stagnation. In fact one leading private sector figure mentioned to me that even though Jamaica has not made any progress we still seem to shower those responsible for its problems with national honours.

This spurred me to think about the much needed solution for Jamaica to achieve the desirable economic and social development. For as said by the present Prime Minister, the Honourable Bruce Golding, given the natural resources and achievements there is no reason for Jamaica to be poor.

During the 1980s and 1990s, on becoming aware of Jamaica's economic environment, I listened to commentaries from many economists as they prescribed solutions but to no avail as Jamaica's economy has worsened over the years. These proposals sounded solid, and many were, but have not resulted in Jamaica's improvement.

In the 1980s various exchange rate regimes were being debated, including the merits and demerits of a fixed or managed floating rate. This was a time when the economy was highly protected. The restrictions included licenses to import motor vehicles and foreign currency restrictions such as the maximum US$50 allowed per trip that could be taken out of the country.

---

[2] "Yes we can Jamaica" - Jamaica Observer, November 7, 2008, Dennis Chung

By the 1990s foreign exchange controls were no longer a problem and motor vehicles were in abundance. No longer could you buy a car and sell it back three years later for twice the amount of money purchased for. In the early 1990s many purchased United States dollars and put it under their mattress, or bought any stock on the Jamaica Stock Exchange, as both the United States dollar and stocks were guaranteed to go up, given the high levels of inflation. By the mid 1990s that changed however, as with a new finance minister, Dr. Omar Davies, the focus was on stabilizing the macro economy by controlling inflation and the exchange rate. Although the macroeconomic stability was necessary and welcome, the change was too sudden for a low productivity and uncompetitive private sector to survive the global onslaught. Asset prices fell through the floor and interest rates shot up, while businesses tried to grapple with the new environment. The financial crisis was upon Jamaica by 1996.

The obvious conclusion is that there is something fundamentally wrong with the structure of Jamaica's economic foundation in its continued quest for economic growth, a fiscal surplus, and the pursuit of macroeconomic stability.

In October 2008 I discussed this concern and idea for a paper with the UNDP's country representative and a leading business personality, who like many seemed frustrated that Jamaica has not been able to make any sustainable progress. My own view is that what Jamaica needed was not more aid or grants, in the form of money, from the multilaterals but assistance in helping to chart the course for Jamaica's development. Even with much aid, grant funding, and debt, this has got Jamaica into nothing but more debt and economic stagnation. This raises the thought that if Jamaica did not have any of those types of funding then it may have been better off, not having the money to squander.

This publication came out of the quest for the answer implied by Prime Minister Golding of why is Jamaica so poor if we have so much. The fact is that despite independence, the efforts of governments since independence, and its natural resources Jamaica has not been able to achieve any long term sustainable economic development since the end of the 1960s. If this is to be achieved then it is necessary to understand what went wrong and what is needed to put the country on the track to long term sustainable economic and social development.

II. **Accountonomics**: My own professional discipline is in accounting, having been a chartered accountant since 1993, achieving the M.Sc. Accounting in 1989, from the UWI, the Certified Public Accountant examinations in 1990 from the state of California, and membership of the Institute of Chartered Accountants of Jamaica in 1993, eventually becoming a Fellow, and council member. My only flirtation with formal economic education was my economic classes at the Cambridge Advanced Level Exams – sixth form – and my first degree at the UWI. So my venture in economics can be seen as nothing more than a regular accountant with an interest in understanding why Jamaica, unlike other Caribbean countries with fewer resources, has failed to see any economic development.

My own analysis and assessment of what is needed to propel Jamaica forward is not based on pure economics but is a mix between economic theory and accounting type analysis, in particular the discipline of financial statement analysis. I couldn't give a purely economic perspective, as I know more about accounting than economics and after listening to the economists over the years I am not sure that I would want to offer an economic analysis and solution only, as it has always seemed to fail.

This approach of blending accounting analysis and economic theory I will refer to as Accountonomics, as I can only claim this to be a hybrid of both.

Chapter 1: JAMAICA'S CURRENT ECONOMIC DILEMMA – DEFINING THE PROBLEM

I.   **Overview**: Jamaica gained political independence in 1962 from Great Britain. At the time the people held out great enthusiasm and hope about Jamaica's political and economic future. In their minds a politically independent Jamaica was destined to be a prosperous nation. I am told it was a very proud moment for Jamaicans as the new flag was raised and the national anthem sung for the first time. Jamaica was still a primary economy then, which depended on traditional agricultural products such as sugar and banana, with growing industries in tourism and bauxite. By 1962 the country had two major political parties, the JLP and PNP. The two major trade unions were closely associated with these two political parties, having either been formed out of the political party (NWU from the PNP) or the political party formed out of the trade union (JLP from the BITU).

Jamaica today has a population of approximately 2.7 million people, and approximately the same number of Jamaicans living overseas, known as the Diaspora. This Diaspora has always played a major role in Jamaica's economy via the remittance of funds back to relatives in Jamaica, as they travelled overseas in search of better financial opportunity they found difficult to realize in Jamaica.

Jamaica is a country of fourteen parishes, with the city of Kingston as the capital, located in the east of the island. In the western end lies the only other designated city, Montego Bay, which has been given the title of the tourist capital of Jamaica. Today tourism is the country's number two foreign exchange earner with approximately US$2 billion per annum behind remittances, which earns in excess of US$2 billion per annum. The main tourist resort areas are all located on the north and west coasts of Jamaica, which are Montego Bay, Ocho Rios, and Negril. There is a move to develop the south coast area of St.

Elizabeth and Westmoreland, and also the beautiful parish of Portland, in the east, that is arguably underdeveloped because of the lack of proper roads leading to that part of the island[3]. The neglect of Portland is symptomatic of the way Jamaica has underutilized and destroyed its natural resources, such as the degradation of beaches and natural attractions.

Jamaica has since independence adopted the Westminster type of political arrangements from the British. The parliamentary subdivisions consists of 60 districts, each electing one member of parliament in the general elections, constitutionally due every five years from the last general election. Even though general elections are due every five years, the Prime Minister, who is the chief minister of government, has the right to call elections at any time during that five year period, at which time a new five year period will begin. Whichever party gains the majority of the parliamentary seats usually forms the government, headed by the Prime Minister. The constitution states, however, that the Governor General is the one that appoints the Prime Minister and government whom he thinks has the confidence of the people. So it is theoretically possible, though not practical, that a minority government could be appointed, contrary to the people's views. The Governor General is the constitutional head of state but for all intents and purposes that position is highly ceremonial as the significant power rests with the Prime Minister, who appoints ministers of government and makes recommendations for the appointment of senators and other public officials. All appointments made by the Governor General, and agreed to by the leader of the opposition, are practically ceremonious in nature.

---

[3] Leading business personalities have lamented the lack of proper road and access as a significant reason for the lack of investment in the area. This view has been echoed by both sides of the political divide also.

The leader of the opposition is a constitutionally recognized position, which is usually the elected leader of the opposition party. The holder of this position is similarly appointed by the Governor General.

The second arm of government is at the community level, known as parish councils. There are 13 parish council divisions in Jamaica, of which the most powerful has always been the KSAC, the parish council that combines the corporate area parishes of Kingston and St. Andrew. Across these 13 parish councils there are 275 parish councillors, each elected during parish council election, which is constitutionally due every three years but have been postponed regularly over the years. From each parish council, the councillors elect one as the head, who becomes the mayor of the parish council. The parish councils are supposedly responsible for the management of the parishes, such as local roads; licences for businesses and certain skills, such as barbers and hairdressers; and public safety responsibilities. Traditionally however the parish councils have depended on the central government for sufficient funding, which has minimized their effectiveness.

II. **Growth challenge**: Since the 1970s one of Jamaica's major challenges has been GDP growth. Between 1962 and 2007, 46 years since independence, Jamaica's GDP grew an accumulated 95.90% or an average of 2.08% per annum. Table 1 indicates that the significant portion of that accumulated growth, 68.50%, has been over the first ten years since independence (1962 – 1971). In the 36 years since 1972 the country has grown, an accumulated 27.4% or an annual average of 0.76%.

Table 1: Jamaica's GDP Growth Rate in Decades (Source: WER)

Range (years)		Total GDP Growth	Annual Average Growth
1962	1971	68.5%	6.9%
1972	1981	-9.5%	-1.0%
1982	1991	19.0%	1.9%
1992	2001	8.9%	0.9%
2002	2007	9.0%	1.3%

Chart 1: Jamaica Real GDP Growth 1962 to 2007 (Source: WER)

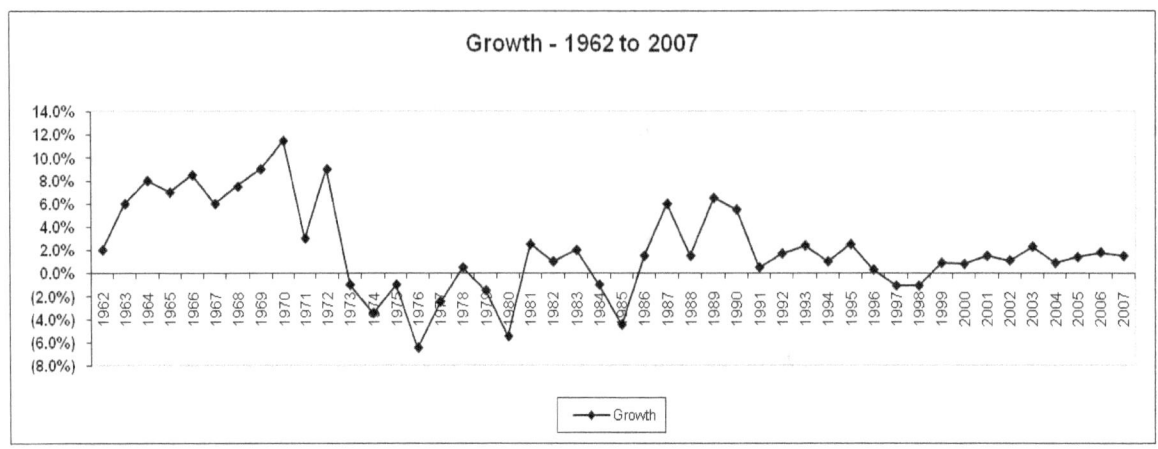

This performance shows that Jamaica has had a significant growth challenge since the end of the 1960s. In the following chapters I will attempt to examine what the underlying factors are that even in 2008, are causing Jamaica not to be able to grow at internationally acceptable standards, or at rates that will ensure economic and social development.

Table 2: GDP Growth Rates of Jamaica versus the World (Source: WER)

Year	GDP Growth		Year	GDP Growth		Year	GDP Growth		Year	GDP Growth		Year	GDP Growth	
	J'ca	World		J'ca	World		J'ca	World		J'ca	World		J'ca	World
1962	2.0%	n/a	1972	9.0%	5.5%	1982	1.0%	1.1%	1992	1.7%	2.7%	2002	1.1%	2.2%
1963	6.0%	n/a	1973	-1.0%	6.9%	1983	2.0%	2.8%	1993	2.4%	2.7%	2003	2.3%	2.7%
1964	8.0%	n/a	1974	-3.5%	2.8%	1984	-1.0%	5.0%	1994	1.0%	4.0%	2004	0.9%	3.8%
1965	7.0%	n/a	1975	-1.0%	1.9%	1985	-4.5%	3.9%	1995	2.5%	3.7%	2005	1.4%	4.9%
1966	8.5%	n/a	1976	-6.5%	5.0%	1986	1.5%	3.7%	1996	0.3%	4.3%	2006	1.8%	4.7%
1967	6.0%	n/a	1977	-2.5%	4.5%	1987	6.0%	4.0%	1997	-1.1%	4.2%	2007	1.5%	5.3%
1968	7.5%	n/a	1978	0.5%	4.7%	1988	1.5%	4.7%	1998	-1.1%	2.5%			
1969	9.0%	n/a	1979	-1.5%	3.9%	1989	6.5%	3.8%	1999	0.9%	2.3%			
1970	11.5%	4.9%	1980	-5.5%	2.5%	1990	5.5%	2.6%	2000	0.8%	3.4%			
1971	3.0%	4.5%	1981	2.5%	2.0%	1991	0.5%	1.8%	2001	1.5%	4.8%			

This poor average performance in GDP growth over the years since 1962 has resulted in a low GDP per capita for Jamaica when compared to other countries. Since independence Jamaica's per capita GDP has changed little in real terms, thus illustrating the lack of development for its people and an understanding of the cause of Jamaica's relatively high poverty rates.

Chart 2 shows a purchasing power parity comparison between Jamaica and other Caribbean countries. It shows that in 2007, even though Jamaica is the largest and has significant natural resources when compared to most other Caribbean states; it is the third worst in terms of GDP per capita adjusted for purchasing power parity. This is a measure of the lack of progress the Jamaican citizen has made relative to other regional countries.

Chart 2: 2007 GDP per Capita (PPP) in US$ (Source: CIA World Factbook)

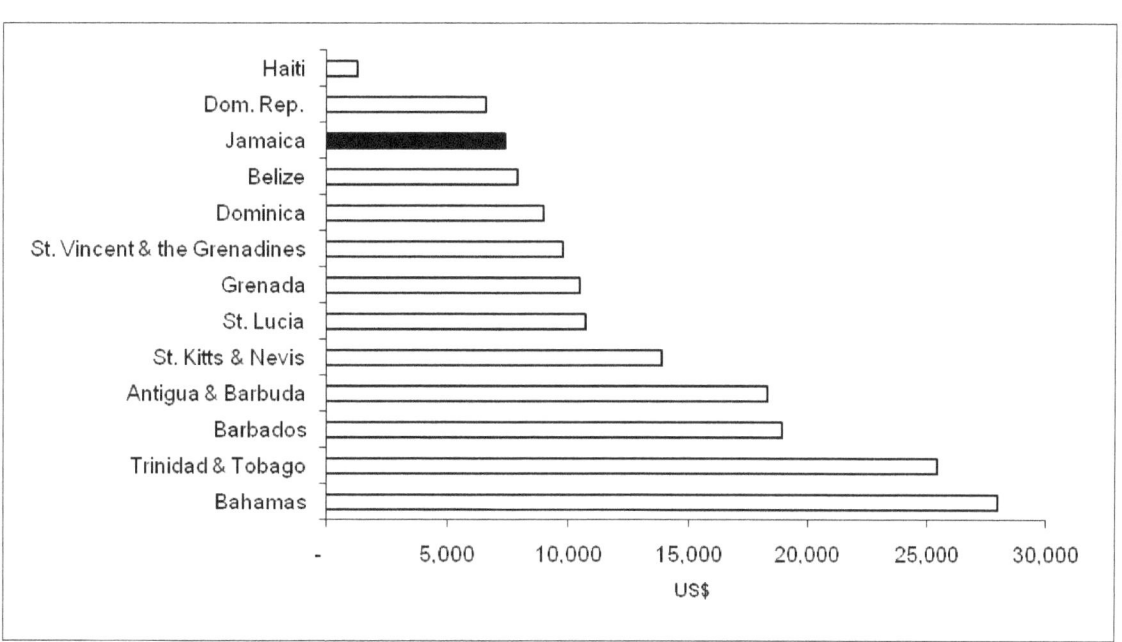

Chart 3 shows a comparison of the same countries listed in Chart 2 ranked by the Real GDP growth rate in 2007. It shows that of the 13 countries, Jamaica was the second worst. Only Dominica grew at a lower rate than Jamaica in 2007. This performance has been typical of Jamaica's growth for most of the 36 years between 1972 and 2007, and during this period it was only in the latter half of the 1980s that Jamaica consistently saw any acceptable growth levels, as indicated in Table 2. It is this lacklustre growth performance over most of that 36 year period that has been the main inhibitor to Jamaica's economic and social development.

Chart 3: 2007 Real GDP Growth Rates (Source: CIA World Factbook)

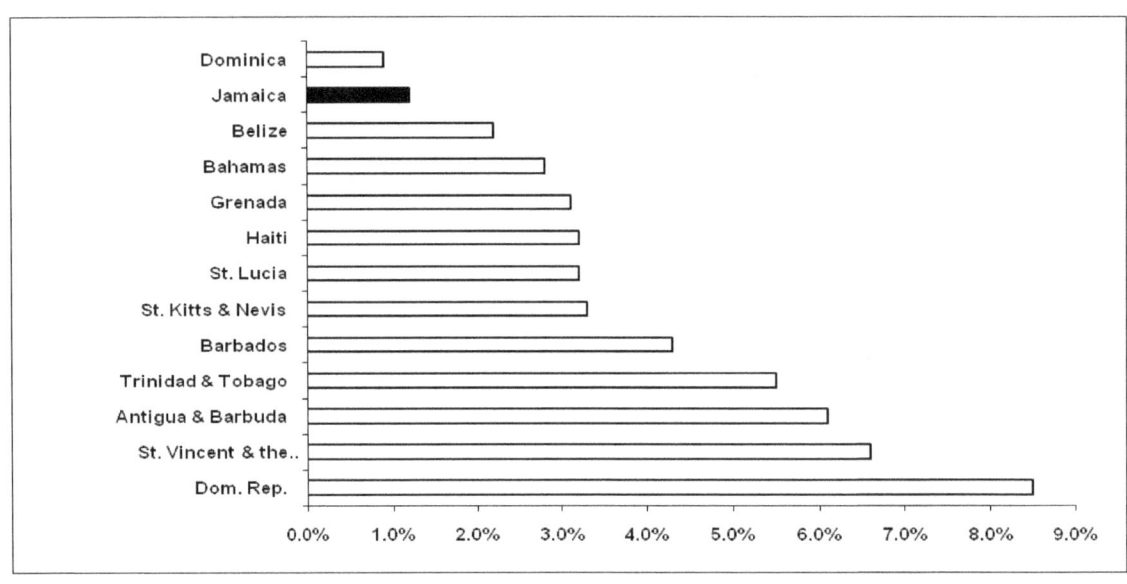

Table 3 shows Jamaica's ranking among fourteen Caribbean countries over the 28 years between 1980 and 2007, in the areas of (i) Average current account balance as a percentage of GDP; (ii) real GDP increase expressed as a percentage of 1980 GDP; (iii) Average annual GDP percentage change; and (iv) Average inflation.

12

Table 3: Caribbean Countries Comparison between 1980 and 2007 (Source: WER)

Rank	Country	Avg. C/A % of GDP	Country	GDP Increase	Country	Avg. Annual GDP Change	Country	Avg. Inflation
1	Trinidad and Tobago	2.95%	St. Kitts and Nevis	839%	Belize	6.23%	Guyana	20.68%
2	Dominican Republic	-2.68%	St. Vincent and the Grenadines	742%	Antigua and Barbuda	4.93%	**Jamaica**	**18.96%**
3	Barbados	-2.87%	Antigua and Barbuda	650%	Dominican Republic	4.66%	Dominican Republic	17.33%
4	Haiti	-2.94%	Grenada	525%	St. Kitts and Nevis	4.51%	Haiti	10.56%
5	Belize	-6.40%	Dominica	452%	St. Vincent and the Grenadines	4.37%	Trinidad and Tobago	7.88%
6	Bahamas, The	-6.71%	St. Lucia	394%	St. Lucia	3.98%	Barbados	4.52%
7	**Jamaica**	**-7.19%**	Belize	258%	Grenada	3.80%	Grenada	4.17%
8	Antigua and Barbuda	-13.51%	Barbados	251%	Trinidad and Tobago	3.24%	St. Lucia	3.96%
9	St. Vincent and the Grenadines	-13.68%	Guyana	216%	Dominica	3.02%	St. Kitts and Nevis	3.93%
10	St. Lucia	-13.82%	**Jamaica**	**216%**	Bahamas, The	2.46%	Bahamas, The	3.83%
11	Grenada	-15.12%	Dominican Republic	194%	**Jamaica**	**1.56%**	St. Vincent and the Grenadines	3.76%
12	Dominica	-17.92%	Bahamas, The	185%	Barbados	1.44%	Dominica	3.72%
13	St. Kitts and Nevis	-18.28%	Trinidad and Tobago	181%	Guyana	1.18%	Antigua and Barbuda	3.71%
14	Guyana	-30.81%	Haiti	145%	Haiti	0.42%	Belize	3.06%

It shows that Jamaica was ranked as follows:

- Current account as a percentage of GDP – ranked in the middle, at seventh, of the 14 countries in terms of current account balance;

- Total Real GDP Increase – ranked tenth among the 14 countries in terms of total GDP increase, as GDP increased by only 2.16 times in 28 years. Over this period St. Kitts and Nevis was ranked number one, at a 8.16 times GDP increase over the same period;

- Average annual GDP increase – ranked eleventh with an average annual increase of 1.56 percent, while the number one position was Belize at 6.23 percent; and

- Average inflation – Jamaica had the second highest average inflation level of 18.96 percent behind Guyana at 20.68 percent.

On the face of it this may seem paradoxical, as Jamaica falls in the middle of all the countries in the ranking of current account balance as a percentage of GDP, while it fares so badly in terms of GDP and Inflation ranking. This can be partially explained by the low productivity levels in Jamaica, as even though there is relatively higher foreign exchange flows coming into Jamaica, those inflows do not translate into high growth rates because of low productivity levels.

III. **Uncompetitiveness**: One of Jamaica's main challenges has been its relative uncompetitiveness, when compared to its trading partners, caused primarily by the low levels of productivity that have plagued the country. There are a number of factors that cause this low level of productivity; not least among them of course are crime, low literacy levels, and bureaucracy.

In an IMF Working Paper[4] (WP/06/235) Rudolphe Blavy questions why Jamaica does not see the high levels of FDI translate into higher growth rates. Blavy states in the first sentence:

"Jamaica has experienced low growth despite the high rates of investment. Real GDP grew, on average, by 1.6 percent a year from 1980 to 2004, while investment rose from 15 percent of GDP to 33 percent over the same period."

Blavy includes a table from Bosworth and Collins (2003) to compare Jamaica's productivity to the world and Latin America between 1960 and 2000, replicated in Table 4. The table shows that Jamaica's greatest productivity and worker output occurred during the 1960s, which was Jamaica's greatest period of growth. Productivity declined significantly during the 1970s and increased in the 1980s and since then has fallen off considerably. The Total Factor Productivity (TFP) column shows that between 1960 and 2000 Jamaica's productivity declined by 0.5 and during the same period world productivity increased by 0.9 and in Latin America by 0.2. So while total investments (local investments and FDI) increased from 15 percent of GDP in 1980 to over 30 percent in 2004, the low levels of productivity meant that the return on each dollar invested was not sufficient to offset the low levels of productivity and drive higher growth levels.

---

[4] Public Debt and Productivity: The Difficult Quest for Growth in Jamaica – Rudolphe Blavy (IMF Working Paper No WP/06/235; October 2006)

Table 4: Jamaica and Latin America, Sources of Growth (Source: Bosworth and Collins - 2003)

Region/Period	Output	Output per worker	Physical capital	Education	Factor productivity
World:					
1960 -1970	5.1	3.5	1.2	0.3	1.9
1970 - 1980	3.9	1.9	1.1	0.5	0.3
1980 -1990	3.5	1.8	0.8	0.3	0.8
1990 - 2000	3.3	1.9	0.9	0.3	0.8
1960 - 2000	4.0	2.3	1.0	0.3	0.9
Jamaica:					
1960 -1970	4.8	4.0	1.3	0.3	2.4
1970 - 1980	-0.8	-3.6	-0.3	0.5	-3.8
1980 -1990	2.5	0.3	-1.1	0.3	1.0
1990 - 2000	1.0	-0.6	0.9	0.2	-1.7
1960 - 2000	1.8	0.0	0.2	0.3	-0.5
Latin America:					
1960 -1970	5.5	2.8	0.8	0.3	1.6
1970 - 1980	6.0	2.7	1.2	0.3	1.1
1980 -1990	1.1	-1.8	0.0	0.5	-2.3
1990 - 2000	3.3	0.9	0.2	0.3	0.4
1960 - 2000	4.0	1.1	0.6	0.4	0.2

The following excerpt from a study done by the Inter-American Development Bank in July 2003, in a paper entitled *Jamaica – Productivity and Competitiveness in the Jamaican Economy*, shows the challenge of productivity in the Jamaican economy:

"One study undertaken by the World Bank (1996) estimated total productivity growth in Jamaica at –0.65 percent per annum over the 1979 to 1994 period. This growth rate is significantly lower than that of many other developing countries such as those in South East Asia which have recorded total productivity growth rates of up to 3 percent per

16

annum [World Bank, 1996]. Labour (employment) growth accounted for 75 percent of the change in total factor productivity while the growth in capital stock accounted for 25 percent. While there are usually problems associated with the measurement of the inputs, especially the capital input, the negative value for total productivity growth, coupled with the high contribution of labour (employment) growth, suggests that the source of the poor performance lies in the labour market."

Even while Jamaica's productivity has been declining, real wages have been increasing. Using 1989 as the base, real wages in manufacturing moved from a unit labour cost of US$100 in 1989 to US$137 in 1998, an increase of 37 percent[5]. While between 1990 and 2000 Jamaica's TFP declined by 1.7 (Table 4). This contrast between productivity and real wages implies one of the reasons for the relatively high levels of inflation experienced by Jamaica during the 1990s, as more money would have been chasing fewer goods. In order to keep the inflation rate under some control Jamaica had to borrow funds, resulting in its high debt to GDP ratio in the latter half of the 1990s.

A November 18, 2002 Jamaica Gleaner article, in making reference to comments made by labour market consultant, Mr. Benthan Hussey, stated:

"Against Trinidad and Tobago, the United States, the Dominican Republic, Canada, Barbados, and Singapore, Jamaica's productivity from 1960 to 1990 fared poorly, registering a mere 18.8 per cent growth. Singapore scored an impressive 386.6 per cent, while Barbados managed 118.9 per cent. ...Jamaica's productivity deteriorated throughout the 1970s and 1980s from an average rate of 5.19 per cent between 1960 and 1969 to ....- 1.36 per cent and -1.11 per cent respectively [1970s and 1980s]."

---

[5] IMF Staff Country Report No. 00/19; February 2000

"...the poor performance was compounded by rising wages and an increase in labour costs...an increase in wages of 1.8 per cent and a 3.1 per cent increase in unit labour costs."

This lack of productivity has been one of the primary reasons for Jamaica's social and economic challenges, which has resulted in its international uncompetitiveness and lack of development. If any positive impact is to be made on Jamaica's development it is therefore going to be critical to address this issue of low productivity.

IV. **Balance of payments vulnerability**: Jamaica's economy has always been vulnerable to international price movements, as a result of its high dependence on imports, and the relatively lower level of exports. The lower level of exports is a function of the low and inefficient productivity and international uncompetitiveness of the Jamaican economy.

The recent record oil price level of US$147 per barrel demonstrated the vulnerability of the Jamaican economy to imports, in particular oil. Comparing January to May 2008[6] versus the same period in 2007, the current account deteriorated from US$490.4 million to US$676.2 million, 37.9 percent deterioration. This was driven primarily by an increase in imports of US$754.4 million, while exports increased by only US$91.4 million. This increase in imports was caused primarily by increases in Mineral Fuels[7] of US$596.3 million, Chemical of US$92.2 million, Manufactured Goods of US$40.7 million, and Food of US$28.9 million. These increases totalled US$758.4 million.

The increase in exports of US$91.4 million was primarily in the area of Mineral Fuels of US$59.5 million, and Goods Procured in Ports of US$32.8 million. In this period there was

---

[6] BOJ Preliminary Balance Of Payment Statistical Update for May 2008

[7] This is the category where oil imports are classified.

actually a decline in Food exports of 2.3 percent and a decline in Manufactured Goods of 35.5 percent. These declines are an extension of the productivity declines Jamaica has been experiencing.

The Balance of Payments structure is representative of the vulnerability of Jamaica's economy to the global environment. As an example Jamaica's inadequate transportation system did not allow for a move to mass transit when the price of oil increased to record levels during the period 2007 to 2008, as happened in the US where mass transit use was estimated to have increased by approximately seven percent during that same period.

As a result of Jamaica's low productivity and uncompetitiveness there is a significant dependence on imports, which have been primarily funded by the country's increasing debt.

V. **Dependence on FDI**: Over the years Jamaica has shown a great dependence on FDI as a way of injecting new foreign currency into the economy. This has been a major strategy of governments over the years, as there has been a heavy reliance on FDI as a strategy to keep the economy going. The problem is that despite the high levels of FDI that have been attracted over the years, this has not translated into commensurate growth rates.

Table 5 shows that inward FDI flows into Jamaica have increased significantly since 1990, in absolute amounts and also as a percentage of fixed capital formation and as a percentage of GDP.

Despite this increase Jamaica has not been able to capitalize on the increased inflow of FDI. This has led many to question Jamaica's capacity to absorb efficiently any marginal

Table 5: FDI Selected Statistics (Source: WIR 2008)

	FDI Inward Flows			FDI Stock	
	US$M	% Fixed Capital Formation		US$M	% Fixed Capital Formation
1990 - 2000*	246	15.2	1990	1,295	30.3
2004	602		1995	2,072	
2005	682	22.1	2000	3,821	48.4
2006	882	28.0	2006	7,801	75.6
2007	779	22.9	2007	8,580	76.6

* Annual averages

dollar invested. During this same period Jamaica did not see an increase in GDP, and has in fact seen an increase in the public debt, and a flat performance in its fiscal accounts.

So despite the high levels of FDI inflows into Jamaica, the low levels of growth and continued need for borrowing raises questions regarding the benefits of the increased FDI inflows. This is especially as FDI usually leads to repatriation of profits, which is one reason given for the rapid depreciation of the Jamaican dollar versus the United States dollar from December 2008 to January 2009[8]. One of the challenges remains translating FDI into significant growth or absorption into the general labour force.

Of interest is that FDI flows peaked at US$882 million in 2006 and should decline further in the near future given the global financial crisis of 2008, which is expected to result in a downturn in the major developed economies into 2009 / 2010. This will no doubt impact

---

[8] On December 1, 2008 the exchange rate was US$1:J$77.8701 and by January 23, 2009 it climbed to US$1:J$84.7492, an 8.83% depreciation in less than two months. Many commentators expressed the view that profits were being repatriated and there were no FDI inflows to compensate for that repatriation of profits.

negatively on Jamaica's economy as FDI inflows do create additional employment opportunities and more importantly serve as a major source of foreign exchange inflows, on which Jamaica is highly dependent to maintain the exchange rate and macroeconomic stability[9].

VI. **Fiscal challenges**: Since the 1990s Jamaica's fiscal accounts have become an increasingly greater challenge. In particular the negative change began in the mid 1990s when the debt started to grow at a pace faster than GDP, having declined to approximately 80 percent in 1996 from a high of 212 percent in 1984.

Chart 4 shows the trend of Jamaica's debt and GDP between 1980 and 2007. It shows that from the late 1980s into the early 1990s, GDP was growing at a faster rate than debt, and eventually GDP turned higher than the debt in 2000. Around 1996, however, debt started to grow at a faster rate than GDP, and by the year 2000 the amount of debt was higher than GDP. From 2000 to 2005 the gap between debt and GDP widened even further with the debt to GDP ratio peaking at 138 percent in the 2004/05 fiscal year and eventually reduced to 126 percent in 2007.

The worsening debt to GDP ratio coincided with the negative productivity factor in the 1990 to 2000 decade[10], during which period it showed a minus 1.7 factor, coming from a positive 1.0 factor in the 1980 to 1990 decade. This would support the argument that the underlying problem which has created an appetite for increased debt, and the financial crisis, was ultimately the negative productivity levels.

---

[9] The move by the BOJ in December 2008 to increase interest rates and the cash reserve ratio, in order to prevent the slide of the Jamaican dollar in the face of margin calls on financial institutions, is an example of the vulnerability of the Jamaican economy to foreign exchange movements. This is unlike developed economies such as the US and UK, where currency values fluctuated significantly from 2007 to 2009 but did not cause the same negative effect on the underlying economies.

[10] Table 4

Chart 4: Jamaica Debt
and GDP Trend
(Source: Ministry of
Finance - Jamaica)

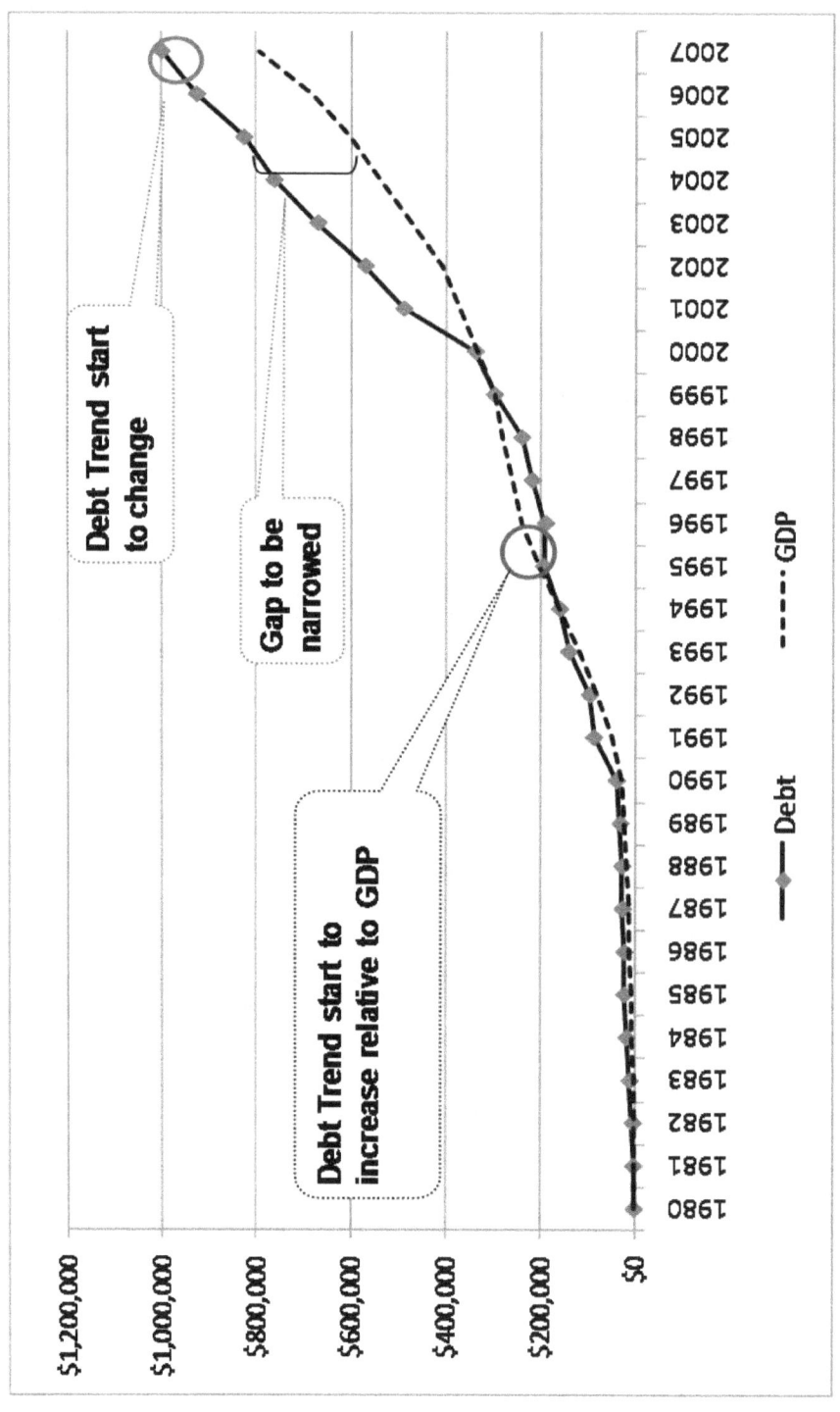

There is no arguing with the fact that Jamaica's 1990s financial crisis resulted in the start of its current debt crisis. That crisis resulted from high levels of consumption without the necessary productivity to support higher consumption levels. In order to maintain higher consumption levels, and keep inflation and the exchange rate stable, the government found itself having to increase interest rates to very high levels during the 1990s[11]. Increased interest rates created significantly greater wealth, based on a paper economy with no real output increase, which led to greater consumption and artificially inflated values. This is not dissimilar to the cause of the financial crisis in the United States, which started showing up in 2007.

The high interest rates ultimately led to high levels of default and a crash of the financial system. The Jamaican government at that time had no choice but to borrow money to prevent a worse crisis from occurring. The reason why interest rates had to be used to curb inflation[12] was because there was a lack of foreign currency in the system and the debt/GDP ratio was declining. This meant that government was borrowing less in relation to output (consumption). Increased interest rates pulled liquidity out of the system pushing economic activity lower.

High interest rates have been a major source of non competitiveness and inability to grow of many Jamaican businesses. Data from the BOJ's website shows that over the ten years between 1998 to 2007 Jamaica's Treasury bill rate has varied significantly from the United Kingdom, United States, Canada, Guyana, and Trinidad; as shown in Table 6. This rate variation has been one of the major points of discontent amongst the Jamaican private sector.

---

[11] Data published on the BOJ's website shows that in February 1998 the overall average weighted lending rate in Jamaica was at 44.54%, which would have weighed heavily on businesses with debt financing that may not have been making sufficient profits to sustain the debt servicing costs.

[12] Inflation got to as high as 80.2% in 1990. In 1991 inflation fell off significantly but was relatively still very high at 40.2%.

Table 6: Comparative Treasury bill rates (Source: BOJ)

		United	United			Trinidad &
	Jamaica	Kingdom	States	Canada	Guyana	Tobago
			TREASURY BILL RATES (%)			
1998	22.68	6.82	4.82	4.73	8.33	11.91
1999	17.20	4.63	4.29	4.32	10.23	9.51
2000	15.33	5.80	5.84	5.49	9.88	10.56
2001	15.42	4.77	3.45	3.77	7.78	8.34
2002	14.41	3.86	1.61	2.59	4.94	4.80
2003	18.78	3.55	1.01	2.87	3.05	4.80
2004	14.20	4.44	1.38	2.22	3.62	4.76
2005	13.69	4.94	3.38	2.93	4.11	5.26
2006	12.02	4.65	4.73	4.04	3.95	6.02
2007	11.81	5.52	4.44	4.15	3.94	6.91
Average	15.55	4.90	3.50	3.71	5.98	7.29
Variance from Jamaica		-10.66	-12.06	-11.84	-9.57	-8.27
% variance		-68.5%	-77.5%	-76.1%	-61.5%	-53.2%

The fiscal accounts for the eleven year period between the 1997/98 to 2007/08 fiscal years reveal some of the challenges that still face the Jamaican economy, and continue to contribute to the country's economic stagnation and uncompetitiveness.

Chart 5 shows the trend of some important fiscal account ratios during that 11 year period, under reference. The following can be concluded:

✓ The fiscal deficit as a percentage of GDP has remained relatively high, around five percent of GDP. Of the eleven fiscal years, shown in graph 5, only one year, 2000/01, showed a fiscal surplus[13]. Without question a consistent fiscal deficit contributes to the need to borrow greater amounts of money and inevitably leads to the government becoming the major player in the economy thus crowding out the private sector;

[13] In the 46 years since independence in 1962, Jamaica has managed to show a fiscal surplus in only nine of those years.

Chart 5: Fiscal Account Ratios - 1997/98 to 2007/08 (Source:
Ministry of Finance)

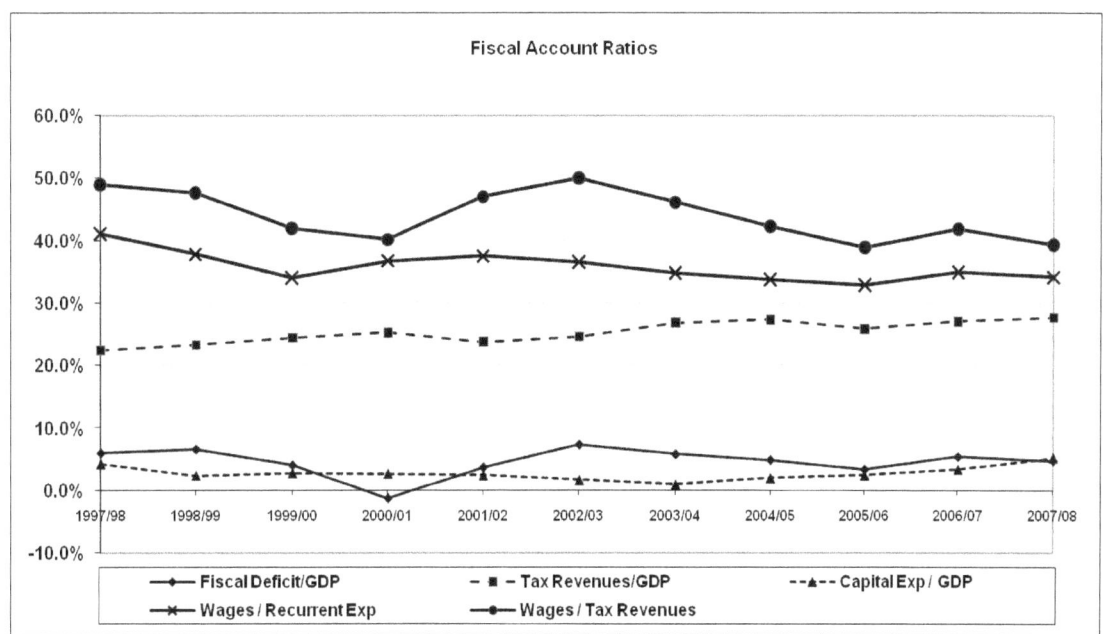

✓ Tax revenues as a percent of GDP supports the argument that government is
crowding out the private sector, as in the 1997/98 fiscal year tax revenues were 22.5
percent of GDP and by 2007/08 it had increased to 27.7 percent of GDP, which
represents 23.1 percent increase in the tax rate during the period. This is an
indication that the government is taking more and more out of the productive
sector, which ultimately leads to lower production. One of the reasons for lower
production is that the return on capital is reduced as a result of increased levels of
taxation leading to either losses or a lowered impetus for investments;

✓ To compensate for the fiscal deficit the government has had to sacrifice spending
on infrastructure, which is very important for new investments. Capital expenditure
as a percent of GDP has remained very low, exceeding five percent in only one
(2007/08) of the eleven fiscal years. The implication of this is that 95 percent

upwards of debt is being used either to service older debt or on consumption rather than capital infrastructure spending; and

✓ Wages as a percent of recurrent expenditure and tax revenues have been decreasing on average over the years. This has not proved beneficial for the fiscal accounts and economy, however, as the increased tax revenues have been going towards debt servicing, which is nothing more than exporting Jamaica's revenues while decreasing the real wages of the public sector. This has resulted in less real spending locally and the stagnation in economic growth that has been experienced by Jamaica.

The fiscal accounts are really a symptom of the underlying problem (low productivity) but continued fiscal deficits serve to perpetuate the problem. Since Jamaica's independence in 1962 (46 years ago) there have been only around nine years of fiscal surplus. This trend of fiscal deficits has resulted in Jamaica's need to borrow to maintain and grow its consumption levels. The problem with a country is that it can neither die nor file for bankruptcy protection (although it can seek debt forgiveness) so it continues to suffer unless there is a revolutionary change.

VII. **Summary**: Since the end of the 1960s Jamaica has struggled to make economic progress relative to countries than which it was better off during the 1960s. Of the 95.9 percent accumulated economic growth Jamaica has had over the first 46 years since political independence, 68.5 percent was in the first decade (1962 to 1971). This means that in the 36 years since 1972, Jamaica has grown an annual average of a mere 0.76 percent.

This lack of economic growth has manifested itself in various ways over the years, such as high inflation, significant devaluations, and a high debt to GDP ratio. On the social side this has resulted in the deprivation of much needed social benefits to the poorer class of

Jamaicans. This has manifested itself in high crime rates, as the lack of money, low levels of education, inadequate social support and poor infrastructure have created a situation where many Jamaicans are unemployed and can be argued to be unemployable.

An analysis of the data reveals that the root cause of elusive economic growth and development is in part due to low productivity. Because of the low levels of productivity Jamaica has faced since the 1970s the country has had to depend on debt and FDI to survive. Even though Jamaica has secured significant FDI and amassed a high level of debt over the years it has failed to transform the inflows from these sources into development of the economy because the productive capacity of the country is very low.

We can conclude therefore that one of the underlying challenges facing Jamaica is that of inadequate productivity levels, which has never been adequately addressed after the 1960s. In fact the policies successive Jamaican governments have pursued over the years have not been to increase the country's productivity but rather to address merely the symptoms, such as stabilizing the exchange rate and reducing inflation. As an example, it can be argued that the low levels of productivity in agriculture was as a result of government policy during the 1970s of providing small parcels of land to farmers under the land lease programme. This set up the present day situation of the lack of economies of scale in agriculture production, which leads to a higher relative cost when compared to international competitors.

Unless the underlying problem is dealt with Jamaica will always experience the economic and social challenges it has faced for the past three to four decades. The solution must therefore be to eliminate the factors which cause low productivity levels if Jamaica is to enjoy acceptable levels of economic growth and move into an era of prosperity.

Chapter 2: GLOBAL CLIMATE AND CHALLENGES

I. **2008 Global Financial Crisis**: The year 2008 saw the beginning of the worst global financial crisis since the Great Depression of 1929. As the credit crisis set in, stock markets around the world fell sharply. Table 7 shows the 52 week range of major markets in Asia, Europe and the United States as at October 30, 2008. The high is where the markets were approximately one year before and the low to which the markets traded down in October 2008. The percentage fall reveals that significant amounts of wealth were lost during this 52 week period, amounting to approximately US$35 trillion worldwide on equity markets alone. This rapid and significant reduction in global wealth had serious negative consequences on consumer spending and employment.

Table 7: 2007 - 2008 Highs and Lows of Major Equity Markets

	52 week range at Oct 30, 2008		
	High	Low	% fall from high
Asia:			
Shanghai	5,860.59	1,664.93	71.6%
Hang Seng	31,897.50	10,676.30	66.5%
Nikkei	16,887.00	6,994.90	58.6%
Europe:			
CAC	5,855.35	2,959.29	49.5%
DAX	8,117.79	4,014.60	50.5%
FTSE	6,723.70	3,665.20	45.5%
US:			
DJIA	13,924.20	7,773.71	44.2%
NYSE	10,311.50	5,178.16	49.8%
NASDAQ	2,835.63	1,493.79	47.3%

In response to the credit crisis central banks around the world reduced interest rates in order to encourage increased consumption and economic activity. The Federal Reserve, in the United States, reduced rates even more sharply than they were increased in the prior two years. In September 2007 the Fed Fund Target rate was at 5.25 percent and by October 2008 this rate was reduced to 1.00 percent, a 425 basis point, or 4.25 percent, reduction in just one year. By January 2009 the Federal Reserve had reduced the target rate to near zero percent and an additional US$800 billion stimulus was being pushed through Congress, while the President Elect, Barack Obama, indicated that the US should get used to many years of trillion dollar deficits[14].

Despite the reduction in the Fed Fund Target rate credit markets still remained frozen and on Friday October 10, 2008, despite the Fed Fund Target rate being at only 1.50 percent, Three Month LIBOR jumped to 4.82 percent, an increase of 200 basis points in only one month, up from 2.82 percent. This was as a result of a loss of confidence in the credit markets, as the risk of default increased when Lehman Brothers went into bankruptcy proceedings and investment banking giants such as Merrill Lynch and Bear Stearns were acquired to save them from bankruptcy. Even the insurance giant AIG could not withstand the financial storm and had to be bailed out by the Federal Reserve to the tune of US$85 billion to save it from failure, and mortgage monoliths Fannie Mae and Freddie Mac had to be similarly rescued by the Federal Reserve. As at October 2008 it was estimated that the write downs related to sub-prime mortgages would hit the US$1 trillion mark, which had been a moving target, coming from a US$285 billion estimate in March 2008.

These events created even more uncertainty in credit markets and investors sold off equities and refused to lend monies, not being sure which institution would fail next. There was a significant lack of confidence that led to the near collapse of the financial markets. It was obvious from what was happening in other developed markets that the decoupling from the United States market that many had espoused was not so, as financial institutions, such as Northern Rock in the United Kingdom, had to be propped up by the respective central banks.

---

[14] Barack Obama was sworn in as the first black President of the United States on January 20th 2009 under the cloud of a raging economic storm. On the day of his swearing in the Dow Jones Industrial Index fell by 4 percent led by a fall in financial stocks.

In response to the crisis, an unprecedented simultaneous rate cut by central banks across the world was executed in September 2008. In the United States, Congress approved US$700 billion to be used to buy bad mortgages and provide equity support to fledgling financial institutions. It was no different in Europe, where the European central bank announced in October 2008 that Euro zone governments would guarantee bank debt until the end of 2009. By October 2008 central banks worldwide had announced over US$2 trillion in liquidity support for the financial system.

In August 2008 the IMF projected that world growth would slow from 4.9 percent in 2007 to 4.1 percent in 2008 and 3.9 percent in 2009. In September 2008 UNCTAD estimated that world growth could actually slow to between one to 1.5 percent in 2009 before recovering in 2010. The IMF also projected that growth in emerging markets and developing economies, which countries have been supporting higher world growth, could slow to 6.9 percent in 2008 from 7.8 percent in 2007. As the crisis deepened, however, by November 2008 the IMF revised its 2009 world growth projection to 2.2 percent and that for emerging market and developing economies to 5.1 percent[15]. This revision illustrated the pace at which the global economy was weakening.

The slowdown in growth was a direct spin off from the decrease in the world's wealth, which caused consumption to decline and hence economic activity. In response to this the world's largest economy alone, the United States, saw over two million in job losses in 2008 while unemployment increased to 7.2 percent, a fifteen year high[16], expected to peak at between 9.0 and 10.0 percent in 2009. In 2008 the US reported 12 consecutive months of job losses, and increasing continuing claims. At the same time the number of companies

---

[15] IMF, World economic Outlook, November 2008.

[16] The last time US unemployment was at this level was in 1993.

reporting job losses by the middle of January 2009 increased giving an indication of the continued escalation of unemployment.

This resulted in reduced consumption in an economy that accounts for 25 percent of world output and is the single largest economy in the world. The need to shore up the US economy with a massive fiscal stimulus package resulted in a fiscal deficit of over US$1 Trillion. The top 10 economies of the world accounted for 67 percent of world output in 2007 with projections for slower economic growth into 2009.

Table 8: Nominal 2007 GDP (Source: Wikipedia, the online encyclopedia)

Rank	Country	IMF GDP (US$M)	World Bank GDP (US$M)	CIA Factbook GDP (US$M)
-	World	54,584,918	54,347,038	54,620,000
-	European Union	16,905,620	12,179,250	16,620,000
1	United States	13,807,550	13,811,200	13,840,000
2	Japan	4,381,576	4,376,705	4,384,000
3	Germany	3,320,913	3,297,233	3,322,000
4	China (PRC)	3,280,224	3,280,053	3,251,000
5	United Kingdom	2,804,437	2,727,806	2,773,000
6	France	2,593,779	2,562,288	2,560,000
7	Italy	2,104,666	2,107,481	2,105,000
8	Spain	1,439,983	1,429,226	1,439,000
9	Canada	1,436,086	1,326,376	1,432,000
10	Brazil	1,313,590	1,314,170	1,314,000

II. **Jamaica's vulnerability**: the 2008 development in the global economy was of great concern to developing countries such as Jamaica. The irony is that while high levels of global economic growth did not translate into high growth for Jamaica, low levels of global growth was seen to negatively affect Jamaica, and further reduced the already anaemic growth levels[17].

The primary reason for this is that Jamaica is not a highly productive society and is dependent on the economies of the United States, United Kingdom and Canada. The reason why Jamaica does not benefit when these developed countries are doing well is because it does not have the productive capacity to take advantage of the growth in consumption of those economies, in addition to the fact that its economic structure is not geared towards development. When these economies are doing well Jamaica benefits from remittances and tourism primarily but these are not sufficient to offset the high dependency on imports.

When these economies are not doing well however Jamaica is very vulnerable as its main foreign exchange earners are discretionary income types - tourism, remittances, and bauxite/alumina. For Jamaica remittances are less discretionary than tourism but are still susceptible to the down turn in the present economic climate, where job losses are on the rise in the developed economies from where the remittances originate, as evident from the job losses in the United States. Thus increased unemployment in these developed economies will undoubtedly result in lower income levels and reduced remittances[18].

The same applied to tourism where it is reported that October and November 2008 registered declines, although for the year 2008 showed growth over 2007. In fact from as early as November 2008, the head of the JHTA was reported as saying that bookings for the 2008/09 winter season were down by 30 percent when compared to the prior year similar period.

---

[17] Jamaica experienced negative GDP growth in two consecutive quarters in 2008 (April to June and July to September) plunging the country officially into a recession. In November 2008 the PIOJ projected that the Jamaican economy would shrink 0.5% in 2008.

[18] In November 2008 remittances to Jamaica saw a year over year decline of 17.5 percent.

Both Remittances and Tourism are major foreign exchange earners for Jamaica. For example, in 2007 remittances led the way with foreign exchange inflows of US$2,162 million while tourism earned US$1,537 million. The third highest single earner was alumina with US$1,193 million[19]. These three have consistently accounted for approximately 75 percent of Jamaica's foreign exchange earnings.

On the import side[20], in 2007, the categories of Mineral Fuels (oil), Machinery and Transport, Chemicals, Manufactured Goods and Food accounted for 86 percent of imports. Mineral Fuels led the way with US$2,013 million, or 31 percent of imports. In 2008 the effect of oil price increases resulted in the category Minerals and Fuels accounting for 37 percent of imports between January and May 2008[21].

The Balance of Payments numbers reflects Jamaica's vulnerability to external economic shocks as follows:

- o Exports show that Jamaica relies on three items for over 75 percent of earnings, of which the top two foreign exchange earners, remittances and tourism, are discretionary income types[22]. The great majority of Jamaica's remittances are from the United States and United Kingdom. Both economies entered recessions by 2008 and continue to show significant economic weakness. Over 70 percent of Jamaica's tourists have traditionally come from the United States; and

---

[19] BOJ Balance of Payments publication

[20] Imports cost the country US$6,459 million in 2007.

[21] BOJ Balance of Payments publication

[22] The bauxite/alumina sector was also negatively affected from declines in the demand for motor vehicles globally.

o The trade deficit has consistently deteriorated over the years. The current account showed a decline of US$647.5 million, or 54 percent, for January to December 2007 over the same period in 2006, and a decline of US$392.8 million, or 104 percent, for January to April 2008 over the same period in 2007[23]. This deterioration in the current account was primarily due to the rise in oil and food prices globally. So while Jamaica's major income types are discretionary and susceptible to global economic downturns, it is also vulnerable to global inflationary pressures through imports. Therefore one of the greatest economic threats to Jamaica is stagflation[24].

III. **Summary**: In 2008 the global economy experienced a significant credit crisis, which is described as the worst since the 1929 Great Depression. There are even some analysts who believe that the 2008 financial crisis could develop into a depression worse than that of the 1930s. The effect on the economies of developed countries is expected to last for up to three years. The global downturn resulted in significant job losses. This downturn has had an effect on the Jamaican economy, which relies on the developed economies of the United States, Canada, and the United Kingdom for over 56 percent of exports and almost 100 percent of remittances. Over 70 percent of tourists emanate from the United States. The implication is that any serious downturn in these economies will have a significant impact on Jamaica's foreign exchange earnings.

On the import side Jamaica is affected by the inflationary effects of oil and food prices because of its heavy reliance on imports. The reason for this is because Jamaica is structured as import dependent with no built in resilience to external pressures. One

---

[23] BOJ Balance of Payments publication

[24] A condition of slow economic growth and relatively high unemployment - a time of stagnation - accompanied by a rise in prices, or inflation. – www.investopedia.com

challenge facing present and future governments is how to structure the economy so that it is less vulnerable to the global environment. One such example is ensuring that an efficient public transportation system is in place to prevent any external shocks from increased oil prices.

Chapter 3: JAMAICA'S COMPARATIVE ADVANTAGES

I. **Competitive advantage:** Competitive advantage is defined as an advantage a firm/country has over its competitors that allow it to generate more sales or margin. Competitive advantage can be broken down into comparative and differential advantage.

Comparative advantage can be defined as a situation in which a country, individual, company or region can produce a good at a lower *opportunity cost* than a competitor. As an example, country A and country B both are involved in tourism and ice production. Country A has an abundance of sunshine and beaches but lacks easy access to industrial ice making equipment, while country B is located in the North Pole and is in close proximity to a country that makes the ice making machines.

Country A has a comparative advantage in tourism as it naturally has an environment to which tourists are attracted. Country B on the other hand has easier and lower cost access to the ice making machines, and has to put less effort in ice production than tourism, and therefore has a comparative advantage in ice production.

It therefore makes sense for country A to focus its resources on tourism until capacity is reached, and similarly for country B to focus on ice production. Jamaica, for example, has a comparative advantage in tourism as the opportunity cost to providing the tourism service is very low as Jamaica is already blessed with the natural attributes and years of experience in the market. The opportunity cost of engaging in the tourism market is therefore very low when compared to getting into Information Technology, for example.

The interesting thing about comparative advantage, whether one is referring to a country or company, is that it can change with new policies or resources. For example, in

Jamaica's case it currently does have a comparative advantage in tourism but this could easily change if the environment is damaged sufficiently so that the beaches are unattractive, through civil war or reaches its capacity for tourists resulting from failure to continuously expand the number of rooms and infrastructure. If that happens then other activities may emerge to have a comparative advantage that didn't exist before, as the net marginal return from investment in other activities becomes greater.

For example, Jamaica once had a comparative advantage in sugar production but as greater demand surfaced for the tourism product, machinery in the sugar factories became outdated and productivity began to fall, sugar lost its comparative advantage.

A country, or company, will always maximize profits in the product/service in which it has a comparative advantage but this does not guarantee profit. Profit is only guaranteed when the product/service is produced efficiently, so that production alone is not enough.

One of Jamaica's main problems is that it has not focused on understanding its own comparative advantage but instead has sought to copy other countries, which are dissimilar in their comparative advantages. Thus the policies developed to encourage various sectors disguise the sectors in which the comparative advantages exist and therefore Jamaica has an inefficient allocation of resources, which is the source of its uncompetitiveness. This in itself causes low productivity, as the allocation of resources is not determined by the market but rather by government policy.

Differential advantage is created when the product or service is seen as better than that of the competitors. Jamaica, for example, has a differential advantage in Blue Mountain Coffee, as it is seen as a premium brand over other brands worldwide. Similarly Jamaica has a differential advantage in reggae music. When a country, or company, has a differential advantage then demand is usually inelastic, so that one may charge a higher price without any noticeable effect on demand.

II. **Resource allocation**: in allocating resources efficiently Jamaica should determine the areas in which it has a competitive advantage, whether comparative or differential. This I believe is one of the major development challenges Jamaica has faced. The country has not allocated resources to areas in which it is most efficient, primarily because of too much state involvement in the economy.

For example, the amount of resources allocated to, and skill set developed in, sugar has not been commensurate with the returns from sugar production, which has racked up over J$20 billion in losses. The Sugar Company of Jamaica, which is wholly owned by the government lost J$1.4 billion in 2004/05; J$2.4 billion in 2005/06; and J$1.1 billion in 2006/07[25].

These losses have had to be subsidized by the government, which tried to divest the company in November 1993, which failed and thus the government took back 100 percent control in 1998[26]. Since then the taxpayer, through the government, has fully subsidized the losses of the company.

Even while sugarcane has been a continuous cost to Jamaica it is evident from the data that the country's resources are not allocated in the most efficient manner. The 2003 WTO

---

[25] Ministry of Finance and Planning, Jamaica Public Bodies Estimates of Revenue and Expenditures for the Year Ending March 2008

[26] The government again announced in the last half of 2008 that the sugar company would be divested to Infinity Bio by the end of 2008 but as at January 2009 this transaction was not completed as a result of Infiniti Bio not having the cash resources to complete the transaction. This resulted in an uncertain future for the sugar company. This uncertainty further threatened the subsidy from the EU, which reported that it would be holding back on the payments until this was sorted out.

Agreement on Agriculture[27] stated that the majority of Jamaica's agricultural land (25 percent) was dedicated to sugar, followed by bananas[28]. Importantly these two agricultural crops are not being produced competitively as Jamaica, and other Caribbean countries, are only able to export these crops because of preferential prices through specific arrangements with the EU.

In addition to the fact that most of Jamaica's agricultural lands are allocated inefficiently to sugarcane, 18 percent of the 211,300 agricultural workers in 2006 were employed in the sugar industry. This amounts to three to four percent of the overall work force[29].

Table 9: 2006 Labour Force and GDP Values by Industrial Sector
(Source: STATIN)

SECTOR	2006 Labour Force		2006 GDP Values (1996 Prices)	
		%	JSMn	%
Agriculture, forestry and fishing	211,300	17.27%	14,021	5.32%
Mining, quarrying and refining	7,100	0.58%	14,289	5.42%
Manufacture	81,900	6.70%	31,254	11.87%
Electricity Gas and water	8,400	0.69%	10,212	3.88%
Construction and installation	128,600	10.51%	25,271	9.59%
Wholesale & Retail, Hotels & Restaurant Services (1)	302,700	24.75%	75,919	28.82%
Transport storage and communications	84,800	6.93%	35,024	13.30%
Financing, Ins., Real estate & Business Services	63,000	5.15%	32,707	12.42%
Community Social and Personal services / not classified	335,400	27.42%	24,699	9.38%
	1,223,200	100.00%	263,395	100.00%

(1) Combines Distributive Trade [Wholesale and Retail] and Miscellaneous services [Includes Tourism] for GDP data

---

[27] WTO Agreement on Agriculture: The Implementation Experience – Developing Country Case Studies, 2003

[28] STATIN

[29] STATIN

Table 9 shows that in 2006 over 17 percent of Jamaica's labour force were in the agriculture sector, which produced only 5.32 percent of the country's GDP value, while manufacturing had only 6.70 percent of the total labour force producing 11.87 percent of total GDP value. One of the reasons for the low productivity of labour in agriculture is the way the industry is organized. The existence of small farms and lack of technological input mean that more labour is required per acre, even while absent technology ensures low output per acre and lack of value added from further processing[30].

Another point to note is that the non-exporting sectors (sectors that earn no foreign exchange) of construction and installation; electricity, gas and water; transport, storage and communications; financing, insurance, real estate and business services; and community and social services, absorbed 50.70 percent of Jamaica's labour force in 2006 producing 48.56 percent of GDP values[31].

So Jamaica's resources are not only allocated inefficiently to sectors such as sugar and banana but also half of its labour force is allocated to sectors that do not earn foreign exchange and rely on local consumption for survival. It is therefore no wonder that Jamaica has always had a balance of payments problem. In order to deal with this balance of payments problem Jamaica has racked up over J$1 trillion in debt, amounting in 2008 to approximately 130 percent of GDP. In plain terms Jamaica has continuously been spending more than it earns.

As if this is not enough, the STATIN 1996 Agriculture Census stated that 78 percent of farming lands consists of small farmers, who are on five acres or less[32]. The implication of

---

[30] It is the value added through the creation of secondary products and application of technology why labour employed in manufacturing has a higher output value than primary agricultural production.

[31] STATIN 2006

[32] WTO Agreement on Agriculture: The Implementation Experience – Developing Country Case Studies, 2003

this is that Jamaica's agriculture output is uncompetitive with similar international crops because of its failure to take advantage of economies of scale in agriculture.

So even while non traditional agricultural exports have been increasing significantly over the years, as a result of demand and the benefits from devaluation, Jamaica's present resource allocation does not allow it to take full advantage of this increased demand.

This is also one significant reason why devaluation has not helped Jamaica to expand exports. The theory behind devaluation of a country's currency, as was seen in the United States between 2007 and 2008, is that when a country's currency is devalued its exports become cheaper in relative terms when compared to other countries. This in turn will increase the demand and increase exports while at the same time decreasing imports as they become more expensive.

This however assumes the following:

- o Demand for exports are elastic, so that as the exports get relatively cheaper to other countries, an elastic demand will cause exports to increase; and

- o Imports can be substituted by local production.

This is not the case for Jamaica because of the following reasons:

- o Two of the main traditional exports are sugar and bananas that are based on preferential prices under an arrangement with the EU where Jamaica could not compete in an open market, so that there is an inelastic demand for these exports;

o Jamaica's exports rely significantly on imports. For example manufactured goods include raw materials and machinery imported from overseas and even the archaic agriculture methods relies heavily on imported fertilizer and equipment. So as Jamaica increases its exports at the same time this causes an increase in imports; and

o Jamaica does not produce enough food to substitute for any significant amount of the imported foods[33].

So, as an example, while Jamaica's currency against the United States dollar depreciated from a rate of exchange of US$1.00:J$37.25 on January 4, 1999 to US$1.00:J$67.15 on December 29, 2006 (80.2 percent depreciation) the Balance of Payments worsened over the same period.

Table 10: Jamaica's Exports and Imports 1999 vs. 2006 (Source: STATIN)

1999 Tonnes 000	2006 Tonnes 000	% Change		1999 US$M	US$M	% Change
			TOTAL EXPORTS	1247.3	1983.5	59.0%
2,795.4	4,592.9	64.3%	Bauxite	56	113.3	102.3%
3,578.2	4,034.5	12.8%	Alumina	628	1040.5	65.7%
177.7	140.1	-21.2%	Sugar	95.3	89.7	-5.9%
51.5	32.0	-37.9%	Banana	29.8	13.4	-55.0%
			TOTAL IMPORTS	2903.7	5650.4	94.6%
			Food	453.8	616.8	35.9%
			Fuels	379.8	1758.5	363.0%

---

[33] In 2008 Jamaica imported more than US$700 million in food.

Table 10 shows that between 1999 and 2006 Jamaica's exports grew by 59.02 percent while imports ballooned by 94.59 percent even while the Jamaican currency depreciated by 80.2 percent, in relation to the United States dollar. Of note are the following:

o   Between 1999 and 2006, Bauxite and Alumina increased in volume by 64.3 and 12.8 percentage points and in value by 102.3 and 65.7 percentage points respectively. Bauxite and Alumina are products that one would expect to have an elastic demand and seems to have benefited from devaluation. One explanation why Alumina has not grown at the same pace as Bauxite exports is the limited capacity to produce Alumina over that time. By January 2009 this sector showed a decrease in volume and price resulting from the troubles of the US and other auto makers, even as the US Congress provided a bailout package of over US$25 billion;

o   Sugar and Banana actually showed a decrease in both volume and value over that same period. This no doubt is because Jamaica cannot compete in the open market with these exports and are therefore restricted to the quotas. Additionally the inefficient manner in which these two crops are produced does not allow for any increased production in response to even larger preferential quotas; and

o   Devaluation, while not providing Jamaica with the expected theoretical benefits because of its production arrangements, has the detrimental effect of making imports such as food and fuel more expensive.

These factors combine to worsen Jamaica's Balance of Payments, which can only be supported by debt if Jamaica is to escape the devastating consequences of inflation.

III. **Summary**: While Jamaica has had distinctive comparative and differential advantages it has failed to organize its productive relationships in a way that allows it to take advantage of those economic advantages.

There is no doubt that Jamaica has a comparative advantage in areas such as tourism and certain agricultural crops. There, however, has been a failure to support and take advantage of these areas.

Tourism has suffered from a lack of proper infrastructure and an increasing crime problem. The failure to support this market with proper infrastructure and to deal with the crime problem has resulted in Jamaica's survival in this market being based on all inclusive concepts that do not provide the necessary spin off in the wider economy. It has also ensured that Jamaica has not been able to attract the more lucrative high end market.

In the area of agriculture the great majority of the country's agricultural resources (land and labour) have been absorbed in the unproductive areas of sugarcane and bananas, while the non traditional crops, where growth has been greatest, is allocated the least amount of resources. Agriculture has also suffered from crime in the form of praedial larceny, which is a significant turn off for new investments and capital (debt and equity) flowing into agriculture.

So while Jamaica does have comparative and differential advantages like any other country, it has failed to benefit from these economic advantages because of (i) an inefficient allocation of resources; (ii) a lack of proper infrastructure and social support for these areas; and (iii) too much government intervention that prevents the market from efficiently allocating resources.

The result is that Jamaica has never benefitted from devaluation of its currency. In order to see the benefits of devaluation a country must first allocate its resources efficiently to the areas where it has a comparative advantage else it will be unable to take advantage of the relatively cheaper goods[34].

---

[34] As an example in 2007 to 2008 when the United States dollar devalued significantly against the Euro and Sterling, US exports increased relative to the imports from Europe and the UK.

Chapter 4: EXPLAINING THE DEBT

I. **Debt/GDP Ratio**: No one could truly do an economic analysis on Jamaica without dedicating a chapter to the debt. Jamaica's debt has been seen as the albatross around the neck of the economy and which by far is the greatest source of the lack of funds for social and infrastructural spending[35].

At the end of the 2007/08 fiscal year Jamaica had a debt/GDP ratio of 126.1 percent. The debt/GDP ratio, although used as a measure of Jamaica's indebtedness, is not by itself the problem. What is more important is what the debt is used for. In 1984, for example, Jamaica had a debt/GDP ratio of 212 percent, as shown in Chart 6 below. After that peak in 1984 the debt/GDP ratio began to decline as GDP growth outpaced debt growth. This trend reversal reached a low in 1996 when the debt/GDP ratio was as low as 80 percent.

Chart 6: Debt and GDP Ratios (Source: MOFP)

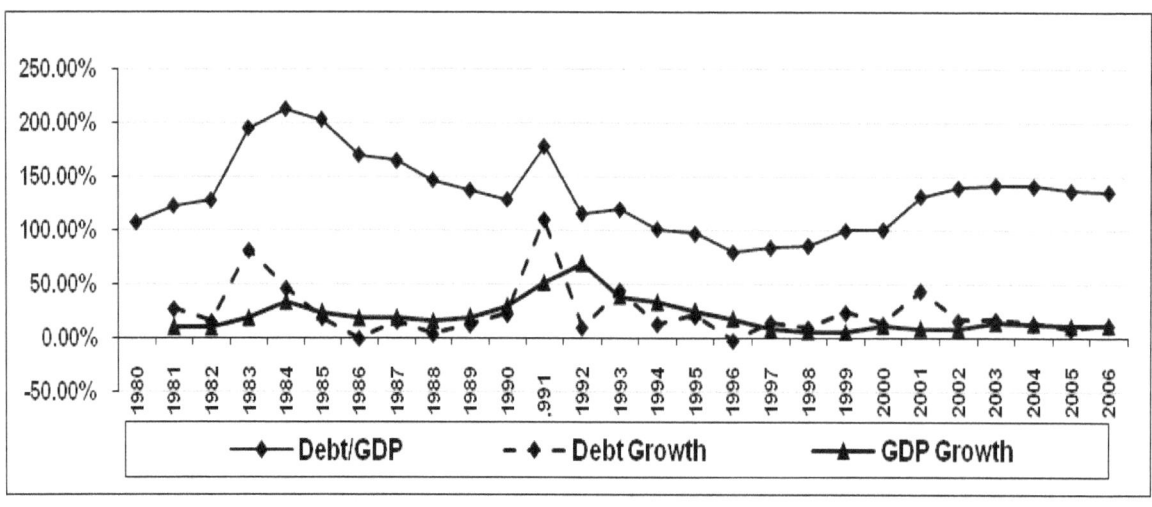

---

[35] In 2008 approximately 56 percent of the fiscal budget went to debt servicing.

A cursory view of Chart 6 implies that the debt in the latter half of the 1980s was used more to fuel GDP growth than was the case since the 1990s, which is only partially true.

Table 11 shows that the debt/GDP ratio has been declining, which on its own appear positive but this primarily has not come as a result of real GDP growth. In 1987, 1989, and 1990 real GDP growth was over five percent in those three years, which contributed to the downward trend in the debt/GDP ratio but the main contributor, inflation, was the same as what contributed to the downward trend in the debt/GDP ratio between the 2003/04 and 2007/08 fiscal years.

Table 11: Fiscal Accounts Data (Source: MOFP)

	2003/04	2004/05	2005/06	2006/07	2007/08
Fiscal accounts (J$Billion)					
Revenues & Grants	149.90	171.50	186.70	211.30	252.00
Expenditure (net of interest)	90.50	106.70	119.40	150.20	193.00
- Recurrent exp (net of interest)	85.65	95.59	103.93	126.69	151.60
- Capital exp	4.85	11.11	15.47	23.51	41.40
Primary surplus	59.40	64.80	67.30	61.10	59.00
Loan receipts	132.90	149.70	184.70	161.30	135.20
Loan amortization	97.60	129.80	140.00	122.00	106.10
Interest payments	88.20	92.80	88.30	97.80	101.30
Overall balance	7.90	(6.70)	23.70	2.50	(8.60)
Debt	693.89	759.70	847.36	923.12	1,000.68
GDP	488.12	551.18	628.52	697.14	793.82
New loans (J$Billion)	35.30	19.90	44.70	39.30	29.10
Debt servicing/Revenues and grants	123.9%	129.8%	122.3%	104.0%	82.3%
Debt/GDP	142.2%	137.8%	134.8%	132.4%	126.1%
Tax revenues/GDP	26.9%	27.3%	25.9%	27.0%	27.7%
Capital exp as % of Total exp (including interest)	2.7%	5.6%	7.4%	9.5%	14.1%

It is true to say that in the latter part of the 1980s the higher real GDP growth would have positively resulted in the downward trend of the debt/GDP ratio but this was aided by high inflation. High inflation was also a primary reason for the decline in the debt/GDP ratio from the high in 1984 of 212 percent to the low in 1996 of 80 percent. During this period annual inflation averaged close to 30 percent per annum. Similarly the early 1990s decline in the debt/GDP ratio resulted primarily from very high inflation rates.

The debt/GDP ratio expresses both debt and GDP in nominal terms, which mean that as long as inflation grows the GDP denominator higher than the debt numerator then the debt/GDP ratio improves, even if the absolute debt is higher than the previous year.

Two factors that would have helped these ratios are:

- ✓ The relative stability of the rate of exchange has kept the growth of the external debt below the rate of inflation; and

- ✓ The move in 1999 to make the domestic debt, of which approximately 88 percent is in J$, greater than the external debt meant that in real terms the debt would grow less than the nominal GDP growth.

So the debt/GDP ratio alone is not an appropriate measure of economic progress, as while Jamaica has seen a reduction in the debt/GDP ratio this has been at the expense of higher inflation while still not achieving acceptable growth standards.

II. **Efficient Debt Utilization**: Even more important than the debt/GDP ratio, as a measurement, and the focus on the absolute size of the debt, is how efficiently the debt is utilized. In other words the measure of when debt has reached its maximum utility is that as long as the marginal return from each dollar of debt is greater than the marginal cost then debt is good. When the marginal cost of debt starts to become greater than the marginal revenue from debt then it means either that better use needs to be made of the debt or that the maximum utility of debt has been reached.

The role of debt for Jamaica should be to generate real economic growth, not just in terms of constant prices but also as it relates to the contribution to the economy. The challenge is how Jamaica can channel debt to a greater level of productivity.

The fiscal accounts data in Table 11 shows positive developments, as Debt Servicing (principal and interest) as a percentage of Revenues and Grants declined from 2003/04 at 123.9 percent to 82.3 percent in 2007/08. More importantly capital expenditure, as a percentage of total expenditure, increased from 2.7 percent to 14.1 percent over the same period. These are indeed positive signs but have been at the expense of relatively higher inflation caused primarily by a worsening exchange rate[36].

Between April 1, 2003 and March 31, 2008 Jamaica's exchange rate moved from US$1.00:J$56.49 to US$1.00:J$71.09, a depreciation of 25.8 percent, or 5.1 percent per annum. However between 1996 and 2001 when the debt/GDP ratio moved from 79.82 percent to 131.74 percent the rate of exchange moved an average of 2.9 percent per annum, from US$1.00:J$40.01 to US$1.00:J$45.68.

This clearly indicates that under Jamaica's current economic arrangements there will always be a juggling act between

---

[36] The provisional numbers for March to November 2008 showed that debt servicing as a percentage of revenues and grants increased from 132.5 percent as at March 31, 2008, to 157.5 percent. In addition capital expenditure as a percent of total expenditure decreased to 9.4 percent. These resulted because revenues were J$13.8 billion, or 7.5 percent, behind target as Jamaican businesses started to see the effects of the global economic crisis thereby resulting in a significant negative deviation in tax revenues. By the end of the September 2008 quarter Jamaica was officially in a recession having recorded two consecutive periods of negative growth.

inflation, the rate of exchange, and the debt/GDP ratio. The real issue is that the policies to attack these indicators as the main solution is misguided as these are merely the symptoms of the underlying problem.

What is more important than just managing the debt, growth, or inflation as a final goal is to focus on improving productivity relative to other countries. It is important that productivity improves relative to other countries as unless this is done then the only way for a country to compete is to devalue its currency, and even this is not a guarantee of improved competitiveness, as evidenced by Jamaica,[37] and can be inflationary. Devaluation only helps when the market is allowed to operate efficiently, which has not been the case in Jamaica.

III. **GDP growth measurement**: Jamaica's problem with economic growth is not just the fact that since 1990 growth has been elusive when compared to similar countries. Jamaica also faces a challenge of the quality of growth; in that much of its growth reside in sectors that do not provide any foreign exchange earnings but rather uses foreign exchange, as the inputs into these sectors have a very high import level.

As an example in Table 12, the real GDP growth by sectors between 1998 and 2007 show that although Jamaica showed real growth in nine of the ten years, there is a problem with the quality. This explains why even with Jamaica's small real growth the goods and services trade deficit keeps deteriorating.

---

[37] As illustrated in Chapter 3 because Jamaica has failed to allocate resources to areas where it has a comparative advantage and can therefore take advantage of the benefits of devaluation.

Table 12: Real GDP Growth 1998 - 2007 (Source: PIOJ)

	1998	1999	2000	2001	2002	2003	2004	2005	2006	2007
Agriculture, forestry and fishing	-2.4%	2.7%	-12.7%	6.7%	-6.8%	7.0%	-11.2%	-6.8%	16.2%	-6.0%
Mining, quarrying and refining	1.9%	1.0%	-0.3%	2.9%	2.1%	5.0%	2.2%	2.8%	1.2%	-2.7%
Manufacture	-5.7%	-4.3%	-1.7%	-0.8%	-2.0%	-0.5%	1.4%	-4.4%	-2.3%	0.2%
Food, beverages & tobacco	-4.7%	-1.8%	0.2%	3.7%	-1.2%	-1.0%	3.5%	-0.6%	-4.4%	2.7%
Other manufacturing	-6.6%	-6.6%	-3.5%	-5.2%	-2.9%	0.0%	-0.9%	-8.7%	0.3%	-2.8%
Electricity Gas and water (1)	6.3%	4.6%	2.0%	0.7%	4.6%	4.7%	-0.1%	4.2%	3.2%	0.6%
Construction (1)	-3.2%	1.1%	0.2%	-0.2%	-1.0%	5.1%	8.4%	7.5%	-1.9%	4.6%
Wholesale & retail trade; Repairs & installation of machinery (1)	-1.6%	-1.6%	2.5%	-0.3%	0.4%	1.7%	1.5%	1.4%	2.1%	2.0%
Hotels and restaurants	3.4%	2.7%	5.3%	-1.3%	0.2%	4.6%	4.3%	4.5%	10.1%	0.7%
Transport storage and communications (1)	7.0%	6.9%	6.7%	4.8%	6.2%	4.0%	1.4%	0.9%	4.4%	3.3%
Finance & insurance services (1)	-6.2%	5.2%	4.1%	5.9%	6.3%	6.8%	2.4%	-0.2%	1.7%	3.4%
Real estate renting & business activities (1)	-1.2%	-0.6%	-0.2%	0.9%	0.6%	2.2%	1.9%	1.4%	1.8%	3.2%
Producers of government services (1)	0.7%	0.7%	-0.4%	1.4%	0.8%	0.2%	0.2%	0.3%	1.0%	0.8%
Other services (1)	-0.9%	1.0%	1.4%	0.2%	2.6%	4.2%	2.4%	2.7%	4.1%	1.9%
Total GDP	-1.0%	1.0%	0.9%	1.3%	1.0%	3.5%	1.4%	1.0%	2.7%	1.4%
Average GDP growth:										
Non export sectors	0.1%	2.2%	2.0%	1.7%	2.6%	3.6%	2.3%	2.3%	2.1%	2.5%
Export sectors	-2.37%	-1.03%	-2.11%	1.0%	-1.76%	2.5%	-0.11%	-2.19%	3.5%	-1.30%
Trade deficit (US$Mn)		(593.2)	(814.9)	(1,235.1)	(1,599.4)	(1,381.5)	(1,379.0)	(1,974.0)	(2,315.9)	(2,993.5)

Table 12 divides the GDP sectors into export and non-export [noted with (1)]. There is of course some amount of cross contamination as primarily in the export sectors they would include some amount of local consumption, which would worsen the analysis.

What Table 12 shows is that even though there has been real GDP growth from 1999 to 2007, the goods and services trade balance has been consistently worsening, with the only exceptions being in 2003 and 2004 when it improved over 2002 before worsening again.

51

Rough averages of the non-export and export sectors show that the non-export sectors have grown in all ten years. The export sectors on the other hand have only grown three of the ten years. The average growth over the ten year period was 2.1 percent and negative 0.4 percent for the non-export and export sectors respectively. This phenomenon has resulted in a declining trade balance, as the growing non-export sectors rely on imports, and at the same time the export sectors have declined on average. This translates to an increase in imports over exports, and ultimately a deteriorating trade deficit.

The conclusion is that overall GDP growth is not necessarily good as it depends on the quality of the growth sectors, as is the case in Jamaica where economic growth has resulted in a long term worsening of the economy.

This can be demonstrated by looking at the relationship of the increasing variance between the non-foreign exchange earnings and foreign exchange earning sectors, and the trade deficit with the United States, Jamaica's major trading partner, as an example.

Chart 7 shows that as the non-export (non-foreign exchange earnings) sectors increased their value as a percentage of total GDP, Jamaica also experienced a declining trade deficit, illustrated by the trade deficit as a percentage of total exports to the United States. This strongly suggests that GDP growth alone is not enough. It is more important for the focus to be placed on increasing the foreign exchange earnings component of total GDP output even if there is no growth. In Jamaica's case growth has been bad for the long term economy as it has come in the non-foreign exchange earning sectors relative to the foreign exchange earning sectors.

Chart 7: Relation between GDP Sectors and Trade Deficit with the United States (Source: BOJ and US Census Bureau

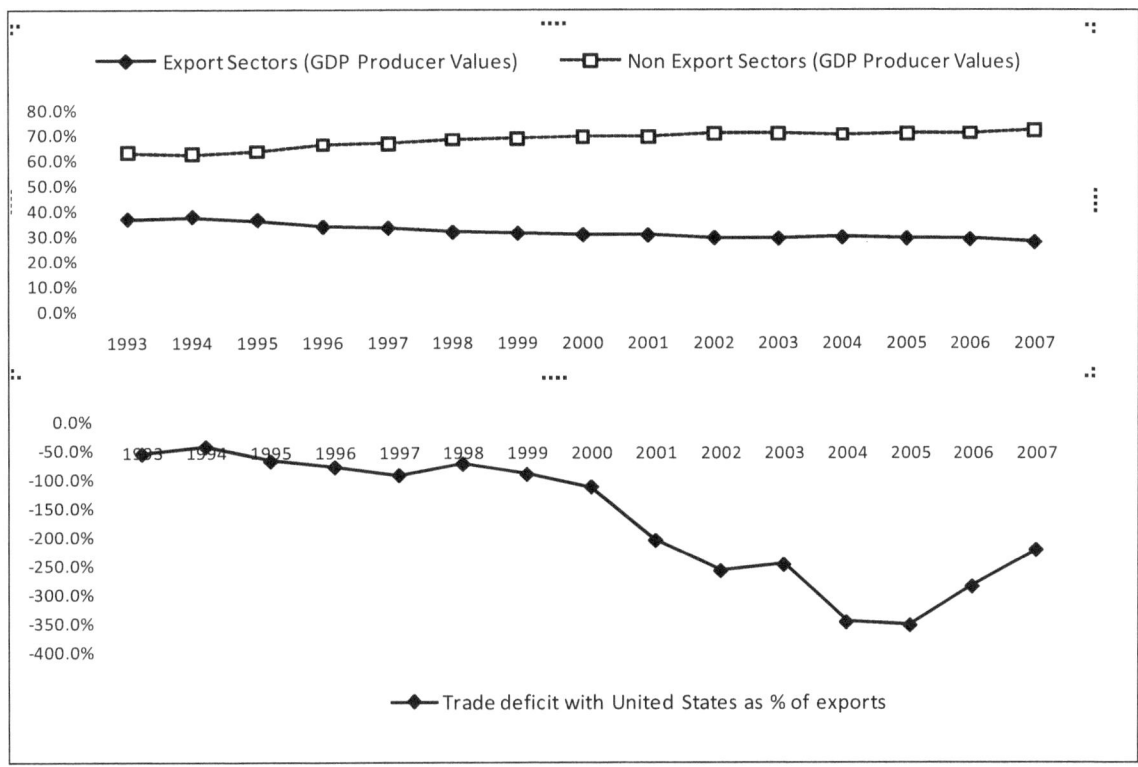

The question may be asked, why then did the trade deficit as a percentage of exports decrease from 350 percent in 2004 to 222 percent in 2007 if that is the case, as the non-foreign exchange earnings component increased during this time from 70 percent to 72 percent. The answer is that during this period Jamaica saw significant increases in alumina exports and tourism earnings. In fact, in 2003 and 2004 the Goods and Services trade deficit improved to US$1,379.1 million and US$1,372.8 million respectively from US$1,555.8 million in 2002 but by 2005 it had deteriorated to US$1,981.2 million[38].

---

[38] BOJ Balance of Payments publication.

The reduction in the deficit would have been good if it was sustainable but it was only a slight move against the longer term trend of a deteriorating trade deficit. One or two years do not make a trend, which is a mistake some make in their analysis on occasions resulting in misleading conclusions. This positive change against trend in those three years does not negate the argument that the quality of growth is essential for real economic development.

IV. **Literacy**: One implied disadvantage Jamaica faces versus its trade competitors is the problem of relatively low literacy levels. Low literacy often leads to low productivity and a low GDP per capita. Low literacy does not necessarily translate into low economic growth, which is measured by reference to the prior year and so growth itself can be misleading when referring to development, as the base could have been very low in the first place.

As an example, developed countries like the United States typically have growth rates of around two to three percent, but this is on a very large GDP base. Countries like companies usually see a slowdown in the growth rate the bigger they are but does not mean they are less progressive than say a developing country that sees growth rates of seven to ten percent. By definition a developing country should naturally have a faster growth rate, and this is a measure of how quickly a country is developing. So it is a worrying trend when a developing country like Jamaica (Table 12) is showing an average real GDP growth over the ten years 1998 to 2007 of only 1.1 percent, as it means that the country is not developing at a fast enough pace.

Table 13: Growth, GDP, Literacy Rates, and Labour Force
Indicators of Caribbean Countries (Source: WER and CIA World
Factbook)

	1980 to 2007		Literacy Rates			GDP by Sector			Labour force by Sector		
	Avg Real GDP Growth	Avg GDP per Capita (US$)	Total	Male	Female	Agri	Industry	Services	Agri	Industry	Services
Bahamas	2.5%	13,001.49	95.6%	94.7%	96.5%	3.0%	7.0%	90.0%	5.0%	5.0%	90.0%
Barbados	1.4%	7,443.68	99.7%	99.7%	99.7%	6.0%	16.0%	78.0%	10.0%	15.0%	75.0%
Antigua & Barbuda	4.9%	6,780.69	85.8%	NA	NA	3.8%	22.0%	74.3%	7.0%	11.0%	82.0%
Trinidad & Tobago	3.2%	6,428.58	98.6%	99.1%	98.0%	0.6%	62.0%	37.5%	NA	NA	NA
St. Kitts & Nevis	4.5%	5,046.78	97.8%	NA	NA	3.5%	25.8%	70.7%	NA	NA	NA
St. Lucia	4.0%	3,402.81	89.5%	89.5%	90.6%	5.0%	15.0%	80.0%	21.7%	24.7%	53.6%
Grenada	3.8%	2,974.57	96.0%	NA	NA	5.4%	18.0%	76.6%	24.0%	14.0%	62.0%
Dominica	3.0%	2,728.51	94.0%	94.0%	94.0%	17.7%	32.8%	49.5%	40.0%	32.0%	28.0%
Belize	6.2%	2,520.43	76.9%	76.7%	77.1%	21.3%	13.7%	65.0%	22.5%	15.2%	62.3%
St. Vincent & the Grenadines	4.4%	2,397.58	96.0%	96.0%	96.0%	10.0%	26.0%	64.0%	26.0%	17.0%	57.0%
Jamaica	1.6%	2,335.18	87.9%	84.1%	91.6%	5.1%	32.7%	62.2%	17.0%	19.0%	64.0%
Dominican Republic	4.7%	2,212.55	86.8%	86.8%	87.2%	17.0%	24.3%	58.7%	17.0%	24.3%	58.7%
Guyana	1.2%	728.29	98.8%	99.1%	98.5%	31.1%	21.7%	47.1%	4.0%	40.4%	65.6%
Haiti	0.4%	354.81	52.9%	54.8%	51.2%	28.0%	20.0%	52.0%	66.0%	9.0%	25.0%

Table 13 shows that there is no identifiable relationship between literacy rates and total GDP growth or the distribution of GDP and labour force by sector. What it shows though is that there seems to be a relationship between literacy levels and growth rates with GDP per capita. While a country may show growth it does not necessarily mean that the general population is benefiting, as can be measured by GDP per capita[39], for example in the case of the Dominican Republic. What is needed for the greatest positive effect on GDP per capita are high growth and literacy rates. However, the best positive effect on GDP per capita comes from a high literacy rate, as shown in the Bahamas and Barbados, where the average growth is below many of the other averages but that country has a high literacy

---

[39] This is because the population growth rate can outpace the GDP growth rate. Even GDP per capita is not a precise measure of the population generally benefitting as growth can be concentrated in the hands of a few and so social policies like greater access to education are essential.

rate. The more literate (educated) someone is then usually the higher the value of output, and hence GDP per capita.

It is therefore very important for the government to focus not only on GDP growth, as has been Jamaica's main focus, but even more importantly on increasing literacy levels through targeted education programmes. This is because while a country may experience exceptional growth it will not necessarily filter down to the general population as reflected by GDP per capita. **This supports the view that improved education quality is a necessary and beneficial fiscal policy**.

In order to develop an economy it is not enough to just focus on the real GDP growth number but is critical to drill down to GDP per capita and ensure growth is felt across the population. Although the general measure for this effect is GDP per capita a deeper analysis of the education statistics is important to understand income distribution. This is necessary as the more educated a population is then the greater will be the trickledown effect of growth and FDI inflows.

This is an important reason why despite Jamaica's record levels of FDI, since the late 1990s, the trickledown effect has not been felt throughout the society. The lack of any commensurate economic growth in relation to FDI inflows is questioned by Blavy in an IMF working paper[40].

This education/literacy problem is one that Jamaica must address if it is to see maximum returns from each dollar invested in the economy, or increases in productivity and per capita GDP.

---

[40] Public Debt and Productivity: The Difficult Quest for Growth in Jamaica – Rudolphe Blavy (IMF Working Paper No WP/06/235; October 2006)

The 2006 Jamaican Labour Force statistics[41] reveal that of the 1,249,100 persons in the labour force in October 2006, 894,200, or 71 percent, left high school without passing one subject at the CXC level[42]. Further only 95,700, or eight percent, have attained a tertiary degree.

The result of such a high level of untrained minds is inevitably low productivity, as education/training makes a person more productive, and if 71 percent of the labour force does not even have one subject at the CXC level then it means that they are more prone to be unproductive than those who do. This is especially true if the management itself has not achieved an acceptable level of education for a management role.

What this means though is that Jamaica must organize its production in order not to be disadvantaged too much by the relatively lower literacy levels. Instead policies have been pursued to provide jobs without considering the maximization of productivity and GDP per capita.

One policy that Jamaican governments have pursued, certainly since the 1980s, was job growth through low value industries without much success. So although thousands of jobs were created in the 1980s and 1990s in the Garment and Information technology sectors, these were low skilled jobs. This had the impact of keeping the average earnings of the labour force low compared to other countries. As an example, Jamaica has looked at the Irish and Indian models for clues about strategies for economic development, which included Information Technology investments as a strategy. The fact though is that both those countries had high end investments in those areas, primarily in the area of computer programming, which was possible because of a more educated labour force. In Jamaica's

---

[41] STATIN

[42] Caribbean secondary school (Grade 11) examinations, which replaced the GCE Ordinary Level examinations.

case the jobs created were in low end data processing, as a result of its relatively lower literacy rates. This resulted in the GDP per capita remaining low, as no real consideration was given to improving productivity through training.

V. **Summary**: While the debt/GDP ratio has been used as a measurement of the debt burden and state of the economy, this may be misleading and is a possible reason why Jamaica has not been able to make much progress, as the focus has been on the wrong measurement. A more important measure of debt would be how efficiently it is utilized, that is the marginal return on each new dollar of debt compared to the marginal cost. Debt can be seen as good up to the point where marginal revenue equals marginal cost, as applied under marginal costing theory.

The marginal measurement of debt is only the start however and Jamaica must ensure that debt translates into growth that has a positive effect on the economy. Growth in Jamaica over the years has primarily been in the sectors that do not provide foreign exchange earnings but rather consumes it. The result of this is a continuing balance of payments challenge, which places pressure on the inflation and exchange rates.

At the end of the day what is going to be important is increased productivity geared towards earning more foreign exchange. One significant challenge Jamaica faces with productivity is the low literacy levels, relative to other countries. This does not allow for the trickledown effect of the record levels of FDI Jamaica has seen since the 1990s, and more importantly does not allow for the establishment of high value jobs for Jamaicans.

Chapter 5: *REDEFINING THE ECONOMIC MODEL*

I. **Economic and social relationships**: If Jamaica is truly to effect change in its economic fortunes it means structurally rebuilding the production and social relationships. This of course means defining a new economic model, which involves a redefinition of the economic relationships between the factors of production – human capital, money capital and land.

It is obvious from the analysis and data in the previous chapters that Jamaica's economic relationships and policy objectives have not resulted in any sustainable development since independence in 1962. Even during the high economic growth era of the 1960s, Jamaica still had a relatively high level of unemployment and illiteracy. During that time, however, Jamaica had a greater comparative advantage in sugarcane, banana, and bauxite production. More importantly, however, Jamaica was emerging from a colonial state with all the discipline and structure that was imposed. Both these factors made growth a lot easier to achieve then than today. After a tumultuous period during the 1970s through to the 1980s, Jamaica removed exchange controls in the 1990s, resulting in significant macroeconomic instability. In my view this was because the productive arrangements of the Jamaican economy were not ready for the global onslaught released on it during the liberalization of the early 1990s. Jamaica was for a long time an economy where the major private sector players were used to protectionist policies in order to compete with foreign goods. And even though macroeconomic stability was achieved during the 1990s, it was at great long term costs to the economy.

Forty six years after political independence Jamaica has failed to change its production relationships, still relying on the same exports such as sugar and banana, while it has failed to reinvest sufficiently in new technologies and research in a changing global economic

59

landscape. For example there is much greater competition from cheaper alternatives to sugar and also larger and more efficient banana producers globally.

Even though agriculture's contribution to GDP declined from 9.2 percent to 7.1 percent from 1991 to 2000, when agro processed goods were added the GDP contribution was approximately 16 percent[43]. This single statistic shows the potential of adding agro processing, as a second stage to agriculture production, which Jamaica has failed to take advantage of fully.

The 2007 GDP values show that 28 percent of total GDP value was in sectors geared towards export and 72 percent in sectors involved in local consumption. From this data it shows that based on current production relationships Jamaica is already at a disadvantage by increasing production within the present structure. This situation is even worse when one considers that over 50 percent of Jamaica's export production is from import content and that even within some of the export sectors a portion of that value is for local consumption. Jamaica therefore does not produce sufficiently for export and will always then have a Balance of Payments problem as production is geared towards the country consuming more foreign exchange than it earns. The result is that economic growth has not been in Jamaica's favour, as the more the real GDP growth the greater the deficit between foreign exchange earnings and expenditure has been.

Under the present production relationships Jamaica will forever be caught in a debt trap. The solution to Jamaica's dilemma must therefore involve a fundamental shift in its production relationships.

---

[43] WTO Agreement on Agriculture: The Implementation Experience – Developing Country Case Studies, 2003

II. **Jamaica's present vicious circle**: 1996 saw the reversal of the downtrend in the debt/GDP ratio, which began the current debt crisis and the vicious circle Jamaica finds itself in today[44]. This is not to say that Jamaica has never been in a debt crisis before, as in the 1980s the debt/GDP ratio was significantly higher than any time in the 1990s or 2000s.

As mentioned earlier, the debt/GDP ratio was actually the highest in 1984, when it was 212 percent, but since then started to trend downward, as a result of relatively high GDP growth rates and inflation. Based on this trend the debt/GDP ratio declined to 80 percent in 1996, at which time the takeover of the failed financial institutions by FINSAC resulted in a ballooning of the debt. By June 30, 2000 the FINSAC debt was estimated to be approximately 40 percent of GDP.

Post 1996, the debt/GDP ratio eventually peaked in 2003 at 142 percent.

One of the underlying challenges that have plagued the Jamaican economy can simply be put as "spending more than what is earned". Between 2007 and 2008 the credit bubble in the United States started to deflate rapidly. Fundamentally what happened in the United States was that Americans were spending more money than they earned through the use of credit, and up to that time the savings rate was negative or near zero. When the credit bubble burst, because people were just not able to service loans, it created a financial crisis and the start of a significant economic downturn.

Similarly in Jamaica, the country has been living on credit, as each year it is necessary to borrow greater amounts of money in order to finance its consumption appetite. This is the problem with the debt, as it has been used primarily to finance consumption, rather than

---

[44] Illustrated earlier in charts 3 and 5.

uses which provide net marginal returns, as is evidenced by the average five percent and less committed to capital expenditure.

This need for debt though comes from the fact that Jamaica does not earn enough to cover its consumption of imports. Neither does it produce enough to substitute the imports it consumes. The GDP sectors can be divided into those that export goods and those that do not export. The GDP numbers show that since 1997 Jamaica's non foreign exchange earning sectors have been increasing as a percentage of total GDP value, where in 1997 it was 66.9 percent, in 2007 the non foreign exchange earning sectors stood at 72.2 percent of GDP[45]. This implies that as the Jamaican economy has expanded it has done so by marginally consuming more foreign exchange than it has been earning, fuelled by the ever increasing debt. We can therefore logically conclude that the debt has been used to facilitate greater foreign exchange consumption rather than earnings.

Over this period the average GDP growth rate of the non-foreign exchange earning sectors has been approximately 2.1 percent, while the foreign exchange earning sectors has declined by minus 0.4 percent.

Given this equation, economic growth under this structure has been bad for Jamaica. That is, as previously mentioned, the more Jamaica has grown the worse it has been for the economy long term, as it has been growing sectors that rely on imports for consumption while the foreign exchange earning sectors have not grown. This relationship has placed Jamaica in a vicious circle of debt, as illustrated by Chart 8.

---

[45] PIOJ – Non-foreign exchange earning sectors (Electricity, gas and water; Construction; Wholesale and retail trade; Transport, storage, and communication; Finance, insurance, and real estate; Producers of government and other services) Foreign exchange earning sectors (Agriculture, forestry, and fishing; Mining, quarrying, and refining; Manufacture; Food, beverage, and tobacco; Hotels and restaurants)

Chart 8: Jamaica's Vicious Circle

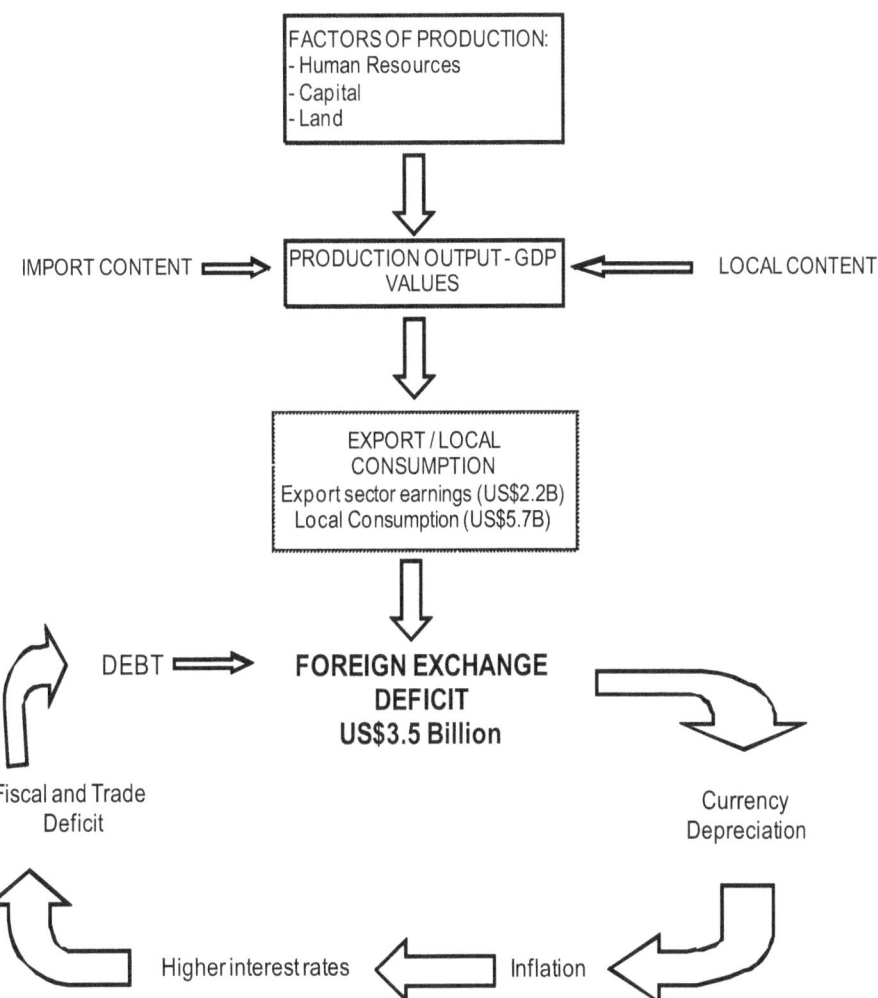

Chart 8 shows that because Jamaica's non-foreign exchange earning sectors are at 72.2 percent of total GDP value, and the foreign exchange sectors only 27.8 percent, this leads to a shortfall of foreign exchange to finance imports. A big part of the problem is that approximately 80 percent of production is based on imported content. Based on 2007 GDP values, and using an approximate 80 percent import content, and an assumed 10 percent mark-up from producers, this would mean a shortfall of approximately US$3.5 billion between exports and imports from the 2007 GDP values - Table 14.

Table 14: Net FX Earnings Computations

	Export J$Bn	Non-export J$Bn	Total J$Bn	US$Bn
GDP Values	159.5	419.5		
Cost of GDP values	145.0	381.4		
Local inputs	29.0	76.3		
Import input	(116.0)	(305.1)	(421.1)	(5.7)
Export earnings	159.5		159.5	2.2
Net FX earnings				(3.5)

Assumptions:
1. Producer marks up goods by 10 percent
2. Local inputs account for 20 percent of GDP value
3. imports account for 80 percent of GDP value
4. Assumed rate of exchange (ROE) = US$1:J$74

To fill the foreign exchange gap Jamaica has had to borrow considerably, which leads to pressure on the foreign exchange and interest rates. This in turn drives inflation and creates higher trade and fiscal deficits. The reason why the exchange rate has such a direct influence on inflation in Jamaica is because approximately 80 percent of consumption is estimated to be from imports, so as the exchange rate depreciates then the cost of the consumption increases.

In order to close the trade and fiscal deficits, and avoid inflation, Jamaica has to again borrow. This becomes a debt trap, as under the current production relationships Jamaica will never produce enough to earn its way out of the problem, and the only way to drive down the debt/GDP ratio will be inflation. The many calls for Jamaica to grow its way out of the debt trap are insufficient. This should extend further to focus on the growth of the

64

export sectors and the reduction of imported consumption. What is obvious is that continuous borrowing to address the problem only leads to a dead end.

The alternatives to borrowing are no better, and may in fact be worse in the short term. These are:

- ✓ Printing money – which will drive inflation higher and create social and economic problems fairly quickly; and

- ✓ Decreasing money supply – which will not only slow down economic activity and growth but create hardships for Jamaicans.

The only way for Jamaica to jump out of this vicious circle is to fundamentally change its production relationships. In simple terms, if the cracks in a house are caused because it is structurally unsound then a paint job will only make it appear safe. Jamaica has to rebuild the foundation on which its economy is based. Over the years Jamaica has been painting the structurally unsound house and not addressing the flaw in the foundation. The longer the neglect the more unstable the house will become.

III. **International Trade**: If one were to adopt an extreme position, it could be said that Jamaica's problem results from it engaging in international trade, and in particular has an appetite for foreign goods and services. The way to address the problem caused by this though is not to stop imports completely but to break the cycle of economic stagnation by changing the fundamental production relationships.

It is important to understand what drives trade relationships and ultimately the value of one country's currency against another. After all at the base of international trade is the relative valuation of currencies. For example the rapid devaluation of the United States dollar against the Euro between 2007 and 2008, resulted in a change in the trade relationships between the United States and Europe. In the second quarter of 2007 when the United States dollar started to weaken against major currencies internationally the United States' trade deficit peaked at US$62.3 billion. By August 2007, in response to the weaker United States dollar the trade deficit declined to US$55.3 billion. Similarly the trade deficit increased when the United States dollar started to strengthen in 2008.

The relative value of currencies is in response primarily to the strength or weakness in an economy and ultimately is caused by its productivity. So when the United States' economy began to show signs of weakness it meant that less capital would be flowing to the United States as there would be less production and economic activity. In layman's terms this means that when the economy weakens there are fewer goods from lower output levels and this causes money supply to increase relative to goods. In order to encourage growth the central bank will reduce interest rates to allow for cheaper funds and increased economic activity. A lower interest rate on United States dollars means that the currency is less attractive than the currency of countries where output is still relatively high in relation to money supply and this causes the appreciation of the other country's currency against the United States dollar for example.

The strengthening of the United States dollar against the Euro, in 2008 to 2009, is this same explanation in reverse, as the European economy has been projected to be weakening more than the United States economy, which has gone though much pain already and is expected to recover sooner. This results in a greater demand for the United States dollar as interest rates are expected to stabilize while the interest rates on the Euro are expected to decrease.

This explanation of the relative value of currencies is no different for the Jamaican dollar. It is because of Jamaica's low productivity of exports relative to its demand for imports that causes the Jamaican dollar to depreciate so much against the United States dollar. This is the primary problem the country faces and is the underlying cause of Jamaica being unable to achieve the necessary growth for economic development. Logically then if Jamaica is to solve this fundamental problem it is necessary to devise strategies that will result in market determined strengthening of its currency, which by extension implies a fundamental shift in the production foundation. The past policies pursued have had macroeconomic stability as the main focus without emphasizing any shift in the production foundation.

IV. **Breaking the vicious circle**: Jamaica's economic policies over the years have not been able to break this vicious circle primarily because they have sought to address the symptoms rather than the underlying problem.

Economic policies in Jamaica have been directed at exchange rate and inflation stability, and the management of the fiscal deficit. These have been driven primarily by monetary policy and there has been a noted absence of fiscal policy. The problem with monetary policy is that it is at best a short term fix and cannot be applied alone successfully over long periods of time. For this reason Jamaica has had to borrow more money in order to maintain macroeconomic stability.

Politicians usually shy away from fiscal policy because this is like the treatment needed to cure the illness, it can hurt. Fiscal policy can therefore be political suicide although it will ultimately solve the underlying problem if properly applied. The problem of continuing with monetary policy is that one day the piper must be paid, and while the world was enjoying record growth rates it might have been possible to continue monetary policy and borrow more. A declining world economy, however, means that credit tightens up and makes it less possible or costs more, ultimately leading to higher inflation and interest rates.

The only real solution to Jamaica's vicious circle is to fundamentally change the relationships between the factors of production and moderate government's involvement in the economy. Government employs somewhere between 150,000 to 200,000 persons, between paid government employees and through their control of companies such as the Sugar Company of Jamaica, Air Jamaica, Jamaica Urban Transit Company, and others. This represented between 13 and 18 percent of the employed labour force in October 2006.

Ending the vicious cycle of debt means that Jamaica must of necessity (i) reduce its dependence on imports; and (ii) increase its foreign exchange earnings sectors to be greater than the non-foreign exchange sectors.

This cannot be done by developing policies to address only the symptoms, as Jamaica has been doing over the years. Jamaica can only make this fundamental shift to economic development by introducing economic and public policies that will change the fundamental production relationships that result in positive net foreign exchange earnings.

Chart 8 shows that the foreign exchange deficit, using the 2007 GDP values as an example, is only a result of the production output caused by the relationships between the factors of production. It is the foreign exchange shortage that causes currency depreciation, which results in inflation, high interest rates, fiscal and trade deficits, and ultimately debt, which has been used to stabilize the macro economy. Logically then it would seem that the only way to break the vicious cycle of debt is to positively affect the relationship between the factors of production and production.

Jamaica must of necessity then introduce both economic and public policies that will change this relationship, and thereby structure the economy on a foundation that will result in export led growth. The problem with the Jamaican economy is therefore one of being structurally unsound, so that economic growth in its present structure, and the monetary and economic policies that have been pursued only results in a worsening of the economy.

Table 15 gives examples of some of the policies that may be introduced to result in economic development (economic growth as a single measure is inadequate), which should result in either a reduction on import dependency or an increase in foreign exchange earners.

Table 15: Policy Options to Encourage Economic and Social Development

Reduce Dependence on Imports	Increase Foreign Exchange Earners
Substitute imported foods with local food production (implies organizing agriculture to take advantage of greater efficiencies and improved and targeted food production) One of significant challenge facing agriculture is praedial larceny, which keeps significant capital away from the sector	Reallocate agricultural resources to most financially viable production (move away from sugar and banana production as presently organized, e.g. the move to use sugarcane for ethanol could improve the profitability of sugar and reduce imported fuel dependency) Focus on large scale and targeted agricultural production to increase competitiveness and output. Must be initiated by government led projects, as in existing environment private sector companies will not assume full risk.
Fiscal policies aimed at reducing luxury imports for a specified period of time e.g. motor vehicles, furniture (furniture in particular should be targeted for import substitution)	Fiscal policies – e.g. tax breaks and tax reform - to encourage export earnings. Must target industries in which Jamaica has a comparative advantage
Examine raw material input needs and provide fiscal policies to encourage local raw material rather than imported inputs – e.g. local furniture or art and craft production in hotels	Fiscal and public policies to improve productivity. Overlaps with social policies such as education, health access and security. Education training must target areas that can benefit the sectors in which Jamaica has greatest comparative advantage. As an example it makes little sense for Jamaica to train astronauts. Vocational training for tourism and agricultural is the fastest way to convert the low literacy disadvantage to productive use, and eventually transform education value to greater output over time.

Fiscal policies to reduce the dependency on oil e.g., significantly improved public transport and fiscal policies to discourage retail consumption. This would have the most significant short term benefit on the Balance of Payments and the requirement for foreign exchange as it is by far the highest value item on the import list	Reduction of government involvement in the economy through: - divestment of assets such as Air Jamaica, Sugar Company of Jamaica, Caymanas Track Limited, and Wallenford Coffee; and - rationalize and reorganize the public sector to be more efficient, less bureaucratic and less involved in the economy

These are some possible policy initiatives, and not an exhaustive list, that could be adopted by Jamaica in order to ensure economic development. Note that these policy options are primarily fiscal policies and not the monetary policies that have been pursued as a primary strategy since the 1990s at least. Fiscal policies are what are needed to change the fundamental production relationships, which monetary policy cannot do. What monetary policy does is merely move money around but if we agree that the structure of the economy is fundamentally flawed then merely moving money around will not solve the underlying problem.

The need for a radical shift in economic policies is demonstrated by the fact that as a country Jamaica has failed to achieve economic development, even in the face of record global growth levels up to 2006. There have been many attempts, not only at the government level, but also between the government and private sector, to implement policies that will drive reform. One such agreement is the MOU between the PSOJ and Government in February 2000.

This MOU was supported by a document entitled *Report on Consultations between the Government of Jamaica and the Private Sector Organization of Jamaica on Obstacles to Growth*. The report did identify the need for Jamaica to grow economically, and more importantly, recognized the inadequate growth in per capita GDP and decrease in net national savings, which are more important measures for progress. The paper also correctly recognized some of the initiatives needed to move real development forward, such as review of the judicial system; security issues (in particular relating to tourism); and improved productivity and education. The paper also skirts on the issue of too much government involvement in the economy, through recognizing the need to reduce bureaucracy and make legislation more business friendly, but did not quite recognize government involvement as a fundamental problem.

The fact that eight years after the PSOJ MOU, Jamaica is still in a worsening economic crisis is evident that either (i) the fundamental challenges were not properly addressed; or (ii) there was no follow through on the prescriptions necessary for economic development. In fact it was a combination of both.

While the PSOJ paper recognized some recommendations that are needed for development, as mentioned previously, it sought to effect these changes within the confines of the current economic structure. This would not have brought the real change needed to drive economic development as it was similar to placing the antibiotics on the surface of the wound rather than ingesting the medicine, when the real infection is on the inside.

It is for this simple reason why initiatives between the government, private sector, opposition, and labour have not borne any fruit and will never do so unless there is a fundamental shift in production relationships.

V.   **Model for Redefining the Economic Structure**: A model for redefining the economic structure for development is presented in the Appendix. The illustration in the Appendix gives an example of initiatives that can be applied and the positive effect on Jamaica's GDP structure and ultimately economic development.

VI. **Implementing the initiatives**: Resources are not limitless, and so the decision is going to have to be made concerning the priority surrounding the implementation of initiatives. Special interest groups will always lobby for the one that benefits them. It is up to the government though to determine the priority. When examining the timing of the initiatives it is important to consider (i) the cost of the initiative and (ii) the time to completion. For example, assume there are three competing initiatives, given limited resources. The initiatives and corresponding economic benefits are:

> Initiative 1- net economic benefit of J$4 billion; three months to implementation;

> Initiative 2- net economic benefit of J$6 billion; twelve months to implementation; and

> Initiative 3 – net economic benefit of J$3 billion; two years to implementation.

In considering which one to work on first we could use a net present value (NPV) analysis. So the NPV of initiatives 1, 2, and 3 are J$3.31 billion, J$4.96 billion, and J$2.48 billion respectively, at an assumed cost of capital of 10 percent. This means that the best allocation of resources, strictly using NPV analysis, is to first complete initiative 2, as this will have the greatest impact on the economy. When initiative 2 is completed then initiative 1 would be worked on, and so on. If the available resources allow for more than one initiative to be implemented simultaneously then both 1 and 2 could be worked on immediately.

The important thing to understand though is that proper analysis must be done to ensure that the initiatives with the greatest economic benefits are implemented first. This ensures the best allocation of scarce resources. One of the challenges Jamaica has faced is that resources have not been allocated efficiently, as a result of too much state involvement. While other countries allow the market to allocate resources in the most efficient manner to

72

gain the greatest benefits, Jamaica's resistance to this means that the country has fallen behind its competitors in international trade.

VII. **Summary**: If Jamaica is to truly break the vicious cycle of increasing debt and a declining economy there needs to be a fundamental change to its economic structure and by extension the production relationships. Debt has been used as a means to prop up the economy and gives the false impression of development and an acceptable standard of living.

This is unsustainable, however, as a continuous rise in debt will eventually lead to a time when Jamaica becomes a bad credit risk, or is not the best alternative for the capital market. At that time the debt bubble will burst just as the credit bubble burst in 2007 in the United States. The longer this takes to happen will be the more erratic the swings to the downside.

In order to prevent such an occurrence Jamaica must immediately begin to apply a fundamental change to its economic structure and production relationships. This is the only way that the vicious cycle can be broken as illustrated in Chart 8. The chart shows that the only permanent change that can cause a positive for economic development is a fresh injection of net foreign exchange earnings, which can only come from Jamaica earning more than it spends. **This leads to the conclusion that the only permanent fix to Jamaica's economic challenges and debt crisis is to reverse the deficit on the Balance of Payments**.

This can only happen with the adoption of appropriate fiscal policies, rather than the consistent pursuit of monetary policies that Jamaica has pursued stridently since the 1990s. Monetary policies by their nature are only short term solutions at best and are to be used as temporary relief policies while the longer term fiscal policies are allowed to work.

There have been many policies and initiatives between the government and various sectors in an attempt to stimulate growth in Jamaica, but these have failed because they have not resulted in a resolution of the underlying problem. The problem with the present structure of Jamaica's economy is that growth, in its current form, will lead to a further long term decline in the economy rather than an improvement. This can only change by a fundamental shift in the quality of Jamaica's growth sectors leading to the improvement of the Balance of Payments.

In the short term, in order to finance this fundamental shift, because Jamaica does not have the fiscal space it may have to continue to borrow from the capital markets and multilaterals with the objective of financing the economic transformation. What must not be done, however, is to continue borrowing for consumption and so the appropriate fiscal policies must be implemented to support this transformation.

Chapter 6: POLICY OPTIONS

I. **Jamaica's Policies**: Jamaica's experience since the 1990s is one of using monetary policy as a primary tool to manage the economy, while during the same period there has been little, if any, fiscal stimulus.

Monetary policy can be defined as

> *"The actions of a central bank, currency board or other regulatory committee that determine the size and rate of growth of the money supply, which in turn affects interest rates."*[46]

While Fiscal Policy can be defined as

> *"Government spending policies that influence macroeconomic conditions. These policies affect tax rates, interest rates and government spending, in an effort to control the economy."*[47]

From its policy actions, since the 1990s, it seems as if the MOFP has been nothing more than an extension of the BOJ. When one looks at the United States, for example, there is a clear distinction between the Federal Reserve (equivalent to the BOJ) and the Treasury (equivalent to the MOFP). The Federal Reserve is clearly the institution that drives monetary policy through interest rates primarily, which in turn determines monetary supply and exchange rates.

---

[46] www.investopedia.com

[47] www.investopedia.com

The Treasury on the other hand uses fiscal policies, such as stimulus packages and incentives, to direct spending into certain sectors to drive the allocation of resources by the market. This does not mean directing the allocation of resources but rather provides the market with an impetus to move in a desired direction. There is a fine but distinct difference between government providing the market with a nudge, through fiscal policies, and direct involvement, which distinction must be maintained.

In Jamaica, however, the main policy initiatives have been centred primarily on increasing or decreasing interest rates as a tool for controlling inflation and the exchange rate, which is monetary policy. The primary reason why various administrations in Jamaica have used taxation as a fiscal tool is to increase revenues in order to close the fiscal deficit. These policies at best can only provide short term relief, as they do not generate any increased productivity or foreign exchange earnings, and if applied for too long a period as the main policy initiatives, eventually leads to economic stagnation, which has been Jamaica's experience from the 1990s to present.

What is needed then is for Jamaica to focus primarily on fiscal policies as a stimulus for economic development, supported by monetary policies to iron out any erratic swings that may threaten the stability of the macro economy.

II. **Agriculture and Tourism**: One of the sectors in which Jamaica holds a comparative advantage, but has failed to maximize its benefits, is agriculture. Jamaica's comparative advantages in agriculture come from the skills developed, the climate, and the flavour and types of agricultural produce. This sector has suffered though from the following, some of which were mentioned in more detail earlier:

> ➤ Lack of economies of scale - some 78 percent of Jamaica's farm lands consist of parcels of five acres or less;

➢ Lack of technology and proper irrigation;

➢ Misallocation of resources - this for example is shown by the fact that 20 percent of the agriculture labour force, and four percent of the total labour force, is dedicated to sugar production, which has for decades been a cost burden rather than a net earner of foreign exchange. In addition, most of the better farm lands are in sugar cultivation. This is one example of the misallocation of Jamaica's scarce resources, which means that with the allocation of resources to loss makers such as sugar the productive resources are burdened; and

➢ Jamaica has not capitalized on the value of its agricultural produce as it still exports its agricultural production in the same primary way it did 30 years ago. As mentioned earlier Jamaica's agricultural production in 2000 accounted for 7.1 percent of GDP but when agro-processed goods are added it increased to 16 percent of GDP output[48]. This implies that Jamaica can get greater value for each unit of agricultural production by developing the agro-processing industry, but has failed to do so,

Similarly, Jamaica has a significant comparative advantage in Tourism. Jamaica's social and economic policies have, however, not been favourable to tourism. The tourism product has been based on targeting the low end of the market and excluding the wider Jamaican community. The effect of this policy is that between 1999 and 2007 the total expenditure per tourist increased by only 0.3 percent while between 1999 and 2006 the net expenditure per tourist increased by 1.4 percent. Over that same period in the United States the average annual inflation rate has been around three percent per annum, so this would mean that the

---

[48] WTO Agreement on Agriculture: The Implementation Experience – Developing Country Case Studies, 2003

real expenditure per tourist has actually declined significantly. In order to remain flat in real terms it would have had to increase by over 24 per cent during that period.

Table 16: Selected Tourism Statistics (Source: BOJ)

	1999	2000	2001	2002	2003	2004	2005	2006	2007
Number of tourists	2,015,270	2,231,800	2,117,900	2,132,600	2,483,700	2,517,296	2,615,913	3,015,358	2,880,289
Total tourist expenditure (US$M)	$ 1,280	$ 1,333	$ 1,232	$ 1,209	$ 1,355	$ 1,438	$ 1,545	$ 1,870	$ 1,835
Net expenditure (US$M net of overseas and resident overseas workers expenditures)	$ 1,052	$ 1,124	$ 1,026	$ 951	$ 1,103	$ 1,152	$ 1,296	$ 1,597	NA
Total expenditure per tourist	$ 635	$ 597	$ 582	$ 567	$ 546	$ 571	$ 591	$ 620	$ 637
Net expenditure per tourist	$ 522	$ 504	$ 485	$ 446	$ 444	$ 457	$ 495	$ 529	NA

At the same time between 1999 and 2007 the number of tourists visiting Jamaica increased by 42.9 percent. This means that in real terms each tourist has been spending considerably less. The targeting of the low end of the tourist market and the decreasing attractiveness of Jamaica as a destination, because of crime and environmental deterioration, are factors contributing to this trend.

While the all-inclusive concept has provided a competitive advantage for Jamaica, despite high crime rates and a neglected environment, it will inevitably lose its competitive advantage with time as Jamaica's competitors improve their own product and replicate this concept. The need for the all-inclusive concept has been necessary because of increased competition in the face of the lessening attractiveness of Jamaica, having been ranked the third highest country in the world for murders per capita.

Table 17 compares per capita murders in the mid 1970s to 2003. It shows that Jamaica was ranked number 10 in the mid 1970s and in 2003 Jamaica moved up the ranking to the third

78

highest. Of note is that (i) Jamaica is the only country ranked in the top ten in both the mid 1970s and 2003; and (ii) Jamaica's 2003 per capita murder rate is over two times the average of the second to tenth rankings in the mid 1970s.

Table 17: Top Ten Worst Countries for Murders (Source: Interpol [mid 1970s] and NationMaster.com [2003])

	Mid 1970s		2003	
Ranking	Country	Per 100,000	Country	Per 100,000
1	Lesotho	141	Columbia	63
2	Bahamas	23	South Africa	51
3	Guyana	22	Jamaica	32
4	Lebanon	20	Venezuela	32
5	Netherland	12	Russia	19
6	Iraq	12	Mexico	13
7	Sri Lanka	12	Estonia	11
8	Cyprus	11	Lithuania	10
9	Trinidad & Tobago	10	Latvia	10
10	Jamaica	10	Belarus	9

This has resulted in Jamaica not being able to benefit fully from the natural comparative advantage of the environment while at the same time, through the lack of environmental enforcement, Jamaica has also been eroding the very environment that provides its comparative advantage. Jamaica's crime problem therefore seems to have had its roots sometime around or even before the 1970s.

III. **Human Capital**: One significant advantage Jamaica has had is its people capital. The people as individuals have promoted the brand of Jamaica through music, for example Bob Marley, and athletics, for example Usain Bolt. The reality, however, is that these exploits have been based on individual effort, and Jamaica has never generally maximized its human capital. This neglect of human capital is evident in the low literacy and education levels, and translates directly into the low productivity and relatively low GDP per capita, as demonstrated in Table 13.

Jamaica is fortunate as the main industries in which it has comparative advantages (Agriculture and Tourism) do not require very technical and highly skilled labour, as much as say high end information technology. With proper planning this means Jamaica can absorb the labour force into productive activities with relatively little time for training, even with its relatively low literacy levels. The disadvantage of that, however, is that the value of the output is lower than a highly skilled industry such as computer programming. The low value output of Jamaica's labour can be improved in the final product by applying capital and technology. One example of this is the application of agro-processing to increase the value of Jamaica's agricultural products, which benefit was previously mentioned.

In addition to the application of technology Jamaica should be targeting vocational education to immediately improve the skill levels required for absorption into agriculture and tourism. This is one way of not only increasing the value of the output of these sectors but also the fastest way to tackle the unemployment problem in any meaningful manner. The key here is to get the human capital on an upward trajectory, as it relates to productivity, which is best served by firstly developing skills through vocational training and continuing the value added training over time, at higher levels of education, in order to consistently improve the skill levels of the labour force.

IV. **Policy Support**: In order to improve the export earning capacity of Jamaica's economy it is going to be very important that the government facilitates this effort by providing strong policy support. This should of course take the form of fiscal policies such as incentives, targeted spending in education and infrastructure, and a reduction of government involvement in the economy.

Fiscal policy must take the place of the much used monetary policy in driving the economy forward. Some of the fiscal policy options that can be taken include:

- Government led initiatives in public-private partnerships, such as in agriculture and tourism. As a result of the global economic climate, government will have to lead

80

the growth in the economy and must encourage private sector investment through partnerships as the private sector alone will not take the risk in an uncertain environment;

- Tax incentives encouraging investments in export sectors. Incentives can be, as an example, in the area of accelerated capital allowance for export sectors or income tax breaks for persons working in companies that primarily export;

- Government scholarships for individuals who work in the areas of tourism and agriculture, with a significant bonding period; and

- Strong environmental protection laws and lengthy prison sentences for praedial larceny and tourist harassment.

Of great importance in providing that strong policy support is an efficient public sector, which will be discussed in greater detail in Chapter 7.

V. **Summary**: Jamaica's lack of development is in part because of the policy options taken by governments over the years. Effective policy prescriptions, especially on the fiscal side, have in my view been restricted in part by the unwillingness of the government to implement policies that although they may cause long term benefits, will have short term pain, and possibly result in the loss of state power.

The lack of appropriate policy initiatives has weighed against the comparative advantages in agriculture and tourism, and if not addressed will eventually erode these comparative advantages. The lack of policies to promote large scale agricultural production, or defeat the crime surge taking over the island, are two examples of the need for the implementation of policies to secure Jamaica's natural comparative advantages. Such policies may call immediately for a guided voluntary redistribution of land or strong crime measures, which in past implementations may not have proven to be politically viable.

In order to grow, however, Jamaica must urgently implement such policies if it is to save itself from further economic and social stagnation.

Chapter 7: A NEW POLITICAL AND SOCIAL ORDER

I.   The data and arguments show that Jamaica's economy needs to be properly structured for export if it is to have sustainable real quality growth, which will enable it to break the vicious circle in which it finds itself. This, however, is not sufficient to achieve both economic and social development. Breaking the vicious circle, as outlined in Appendix 1, and applying the necessary policy prescriptions can assist to achieve total economic development. In order to also achieve social development, policy options must not only be geared at developing the macro economy but must of necessity include a focus on developing the human capital across society.

The implementation of policies to properly restructure the economy and society for economic and social development takes political will, which has been inhibited by the current Westminster system of government. Therefore, before any significant and sustainable progress can be made Jamaica must first define and implement a new political and social order suited to its size and cultural practices.

II. **Relative Social Development Challenges**: Comparing 1960s Jamaica to today, and the access to opportunities and living conditions for the average Jamaican, there has been definite improvement. Many of these improvements have come about as a result of deliberate policy actions, and some by natural progression in the global environment. In fact the 1970s could be seen as a period of a social revolution, in more ways than one. We have seen significant housing developments, improvement in the quality of life, and even improvements in the legislative protection of fundamental human rights, despite not being practically achieved.

However, social development cannot be viewed in isolation from the rest of the world. In particular it is important to compare the relative development in the social well being of Jamaicans to the citizens of other countries within the region. This can be appropriately measured by the Human Development Index (HDI)[49] as measured annually by the UNDP.

Table 18: UNDP Selected HDI Index trends - 1975 to 2005 (Source: http://hdrstats.undp.org/buildtables)

		Human development index (trends)						
Rank	Country	1975	1980	1985	1990	1995	2000	2005
High Human Development								
31	Barbados	..	..	..	..	..	..	0.892
48	Costa Rica	0.746	0.772	0.774	0.794	0.814	0.83	0.846
49	Bahamas	..	0.809	0.822	0.831	0.82	0.825	0.845
51	Cuba	..	..	..	..	..	..	0.838
54	Saint Kitts and Nevis	..	..	..	..	..	..	0.821
57	Antigua and Barbuda	..	..	..	..	..	..	0.815
59	Trinidad and Tobago	0.756	0.784	0.782	0.784	0.785	0.796	0.814
Medium Human Development								
71	Dominica	..	..	..	..	..	..	0.798
72	Saint Lucia	..	..	..	..	..	..	0.795
79	Dominican Republic	0.628	0.66	0.684	0.697	0.723	0.757	0.779
80	Belize	..	0.712	0.718	0.75	0.777	0.795	0.778
85	Suriname	..	..	..	..	..	..	0.774
93	Saint Vincent and the Grenadines	..	..	..	..	..	..	0.761
97	Guyana	0.682	0.684	0.675	0.679	0.699	0.722	0.750
101	Jamaica	0.686	0.689	0.69	0.713	0.728	0.744	0.736
146	Haiti	..	0.442	0.462	0.472	0.487	..	0.529

---

[49] The **Human Development Index** (**HDI**) is an index combining normalized measures of life expectancy, literacy, educational attainment, and GDP per capita for countries worldwide. It is claimed as a standard means of measuring human development — a concept that, according to the United Nations Development Program (UNDP), refers to the process of widening the options of persons, giving them greater opportunities for education, health care, income, employment, etc. The basic use of HDI is to rank countries by level of "human development", which usually also implies to determine whether a country is a developed, developing, or underdeveloped country – **Wikipedia, the online encyclopedia**

The UNDP website[50] shows the data for the Human Development Report published since 1975. Table 18 shows that of 101 countries surveyed in 1975, Jamaica rank 39th, or was in the top 39 percent with a HDI of 0.686. Of five other countries in the region at the time, Jamaica was located in the middle, scoring better than Guyana and the Dominican Republic. By 2005, however, Jamaica was ranked 101st of 177 countries with a HDI of 0.736 or in the top 57 percent. So while the absolute HDI shows an improvement from 0.686 to 0.736 for Jamaica, the other countries have progressed at a far greater pace to the point where Guyana and the Dominican Republic are now ranked higher.

In fact of 15 other regional countries surveyed, Jamaica was ranked higher than only Haiti, as illustrated in Table 18. So relative to other countries in the region Jamaica has progressed at a much lower rate.

The data clearly shows that the improvement in Jamaica's HDI has been at a slower rate than the average for the other 15 regional countries. Extrapolating the rate of increase, it shows that between 1975 and 2005, the HDI average increased by 12.3 percent, while Jamaica's increased by 7.2 percent[51].

The point to note is that when one speaks about social development it is very important to consider relative development to similar countries. This is so because quality of life will always be measured relative to what is available in new technology and the quality of life in other countries. So even though Jamaica has seen absolute improvement in social development, as measured by the HDI, relative to similar regional countries there has been no improvement. The implication is that the average citizen in every other regional country except Haiti has seen an improved quality of life, when compared to Jamaica. This is one

---

[50] http://hdrstats.undp.org

[51] This compares the average of the 5 countries surveyed in 1975 versus the average of the 16 countries surveyed in 2005

of the driving forces why Jamaicans are attracted to the United States, as they see the quality of life there as better.

It is obvious therefore that Jamaica has not only performed poorly in the area of economic development but also in terms of social development, relative to other Caribbean countries.

If Jamaica is to improve its social development, relative to other countries, then one measurement that must improve is the GDP per capita, as this gives an indication of what the average earnings are for Jamaicans. From the UNDP's Human Development Report 2007/08 it can be implied that one determinant of GDP per capita is literacy[52]. An extraction from the data in the report, shown in Table 19, illustrates the GDP per capita level has a strong correlation with adult literacy levels. The data shows clearly that adult literacy rates above the 60 to 69.9 percent range show a wide disparity in average GDP per capita. This is expected as below a certain level of literacy one would not see much difference in output value but as literacy improves the marginal return of the output at higher literacy levels increases. This would result in higher earnings and hence higher GDP per capita.

Table 19: GlobalAdult Literacy and Average GDP (Source: UNDP Human development Report 2007/08)

Adult literacy rate range (% aged 15 and above) 1995-2005	Average GDP per capita (PPP US$) 2005
20.0 - 29.9	1,354
30.0 - 39.9	1,207
40.0 - 49.9	1,656
50.0 - 59.9	2,069
60.0 - 69.9	2,126
70.0 - 79.9	3,744
80.0 - 89.9	9,228
90.0 - 100.0	16,797

It could be implied from this that one fundamental way to achieve social development, with respect to equality of earning power, is to improve access to higher quality education/training for all Jamaicans.

---

[52] Human Development Report 2007/08 Table 1

The Human Development Report[53] also shows that a more even distribution of wealth also positively correlates to a higher level of GDP per capita. Table 20 shows the correlation between income distribution and GDP per capita. The table shows that the top ten countries, in terms of HDI ranking, have a more equal distribution of income between rich and poor compared to the five regional countries shown in the table. These top ten countries also have relatively higher literacy rates. One could therefore argue that improving the literacy rate, through education/training, improves the earning power across the population, attracts more high value investments, and inevitably leads to a greater GDP per capita. This results in a higher quality of life for all, which ultimately leads to greater social development.

Table 20: Income Distribution (Source: Human Development Report 2007/08)

HDI Rank		Survey year	Share of income or expenditure (%)				GDP per capita (PPP US$) 2005
			Poorest 10%	Poorest 20%	Richest 20%	Richest 10%	
1	Iceland	..	..	..	..	..	36,510
2	Norway	2000	3.9	9.6	37.2	23.4	41,420
3	Australia	1994	2.0	5.9	41.3	25.4	31,794
4	Canada	2000	2.6	7.2	39.9	24.8	33,375
5	Ireland	2000	2.9	7.4	42.0	27.2	38,505
6	Sweden	2000	3.6	9.1	36.6	22.2	32,526
7	Switzerland	2000	2.9	7.6	41.3	25.9	35,633
8	Japan	1993	4.8	10.6	35.7	21.7	31,297
9	Netherlands	1999	2.5	7.6	38.7	22.9	32,684
10	France	1995	2.8	7.2	40.2	25.1	30,386
48	Costa Rica	2003	1.0	3.5	54.1	37.4	10,180
59	Trinidad & Tobago	1992	2.2	5.9	44.9	28.8	14,603
79	Dominican Republic	2004	1.4	4.0	56.7	41.1	8,217
101	Jamaica	2004	2.1	5.3	51.6	35.8	4,291
146	Haiti	2001	0.7	2.4	63.4	47.7	1,663

[53] Human Development Report 2007/08 Table 15

Table 21 compares 17 regional countries, including Jamaica, with respect to HDI ranking, GDP per capita, annual growth, and public education on expenditure. This table again shows the relationship between literacy and GDP per capita, and shows, as mentioned before, no direct correlation between literacy levels and growth. This is because a country can experience growth even while most of the population is not benefiting, as is the case in Jamaica where there has been record amounts of FDI without the trickledown effect expected[54]. The table also shows a strong positive correlation between literacy level and the HDI. The data also implies that the absolute amount of money spent on education is not necessarily a direct determinant of literacy levels, as Jamaica has been spending a greater percentage of GDP on education than six of the 15 countries ranked higher in both the 1991 and 2002-05 periods, and more than seven of the 15 countries in the 2002-05 period. So although Jamaica has been spending at the median rate of the comparative countries the results in terms of literacy rate and GDP per capita have been much lower. In other words the marginal return on each dollar spent has been less than in the comparative countries.

---

[54] As mentioned in Chapter 1 under the section "Dependence on FDI"

Table 21: Regional Countries - Human Development Measurements (Source: Human development report 2007/08)

	Annual growth rate (%)		GDP per capita (PPP US$)	Adult literacy rate (% aged 15 and above)	Human Development Index (HDI) value	Public expenditure on education (% of GDP)	
	1975-2005	1990-2005	2005	1995-2005	2005	1991	2002-05
Barbados	1.3	1.5	17,297	99.0	0.892	7.8	6.9
Costa Rica	1.5	2.3	10,180	94.9	0.846	3.4	4.9
Bahamas	1.3	0.4	18,380	99.0	0.845	3.7	3.6
Cuba	..	3.5	6,000	99.8	0.838	9.7	9.8
Saint Kitts & Nevis	4.9	2.9	13,307	97.8	0.821	2.7	9.3
Antigua & Barbuda	3.7	1.5	12,500	85.8	0.815	..	3.8
Trinidad & Tobago	0.6	4.3	14,603	98.4	0.814	4.1	4.2
Dominica	3.1	1.3	6,393	88.0	0.798	..	5.0
Saint Lucia	3.6	0.9	6,707	94.8	0.795	..	5.8
Dominican Republic	2.1	3.9	8,217	87.0	0.779	..	1.8
Belize	3.1	2.3	7,109	75.1	0.778	4.6	5.4
Grenada	3.4	2.5	7,843	96.0	0.777	4.9	5.2
Suriname	-0.5	1.1	7,722	89.6	0.774	5.9	..
Saint Vincent & the Grenadines	3.2	1.6	6,568	88.1	0.761	5.9	8.2
Guyana	0.9	3.2	4,508	99.0	0.750	2.2	8.5
Jamaica	1.0	0.7	4,291	79.9	0.736	4.5	5.3
Haiti	-2.2	-2.0	1,663	54.8	0.529	1.4	..

The implication is that absolute expenditure alone is not a determinant of high literacy levels, as the quality of the education product and access to education are critical factors also. It is for this reason that merely allocating more funds in the national budget is not enough by itself, as is illustrated by the fact that higher allocations of GDP to education expenditure has not produced the needed improvement in literacy levels for Jamaica, as shown in Table 21. The measurement of the return, in terms of quality of education delivered is critical, and must be a component of the education strategy.

The Human Development Report 2007/08 shows that Jamaica does not fare badly when compared to Latin America and the Caribbean, with respect to the 2005 net primary and secondary enrolment at 90 percent and 78 percent respectively. This compares favourably with the Latin America and Caribbean region of 94 percent and 68 percent respectively.

When a comparison is done between countries at different income levels it shows that there is a stark difference in enrolment rates, which could explain the high literacy rates of high income countries when compared to middle and low income[55]. In 2005, the net enrolment rates at the primary and secondary levels were as in Table 22.

Table 22: 2005 Primary and secondary Enrolment by Country Income (Source: Human Development Report 2007/08)

	2005 Net Primary Enrolment Rate (%)	2005 Net Secondary Enrolment Rate (%)
High Income Countries	95	91
Middle Income Countries	93	70
Low Income Countries	..	40

This data clearly shows that high income countries have a higher enrolment rate than middle and low income countries, particularly at the secondary level[56]. This could explain the higher literacy rates for higher income countries, and hence the much larger GDP per capita and more evenly distributed incomes. This does not imply that the state distributes the income directly but that by virtue of policies geared towards access to and the quality of education that this results in a more literate work force and provide people with the opportunity to earn more, as a greater literacy level implies greater output value, and more high end investments (local and foreign).

---

[55] Human Development Report 2007/08 Table 12

[56] One question that could be asked is which came first, greater income or higher enrolment

Jamaica's challenge with training does not stop at access and quality, however, but also relates to attendance. The 2006 Economic and Social Survey[57], reports that in the 2005/06 year average daily attendance of students enrolled at primary and secondary schools was 72.1 percent and 73.6 percent respectively. This attendance rate could partially explain the 2006 labour statistic that over 70 percent of the labour force did not pass even one subject at secondary level[58].

So the data shows that literacy level is closely linked to GDP per capita, evidenced by Tables 19 and 20. It is also evident that a more literate population is positively correlated to a higher HDI, which could be explained by the fact that the population is more aware and ensures that the country's strategic direction is more about human development through the political process. What this means for Jamaica is that addressing the quality of education and attendance must be a priority for long term social development, and as a consequence economic progress.

III. **Social policies**: In order for Jamaica to achieve social development it is of course first necessary, but not sufficient, to have real economic development. This does not mean a redistribution of income, as happens under political systems like communism and extreme socialism. The market must still be the primary means of efficiently allocating resources. It can be argued that even though Jamaica has professed, since the 1980s, to have a market economy it more resembles the definition of a socialist economy. The market has never really been able to work effectively because of the high levels of state intervention.

---

[57] Economic and Social Survey Jamaica 2006 – Planning Institute of Jamaica

[58] The Labour Force 2006 - STATIN

The definition of socialism includes *"...state or collective ownership and **administration of the means of production**."*[59] Throughout the years Jamaica's state has primarily been the driver of resources. For example in the 1980s the exchange and import control restrictions determined how resources were utilized and during the 1990s the state control increased with the birth of FINSAC, when the public sector bureaucracy took over many of the private sector resources.

It could be argued that even though Jamaica professed to move away from democratic socialism of the 1970s, it did not successfully do so even during the 1980s and 1990s as the state still had significant influence over the allocation of resources. In the 1990s Jamaica professed to liberalize the economy. The only real liberalization that took place was the removal of exchange rate controls and some import restrictions. There was however still protection of the local players in the market, and some sectors like sugar and banana have never really competed globally as they have been kept alive through (i) the preferential market arrangements with the European Union and (ii) public resources. As a matter of fact the introduction of a high interest rate policy in the 1990s was only a substitute for the former protectionist policies of the 1970s and 1980s, as government allowed the local companies to earn easy paper money via interest rates just as in earlier years this was done through protectionism. So even though government attempted to liberalize the economy in the 1990s it merely swapped the protectionist policies of the pre-1990s for easy money policies. This could be seen as more devastating to the economy as rather than encourage production it created a paper based economy.

Throughout governments, the political will has never been there to truly liberalize and allow the market to adjust, as is needed for the real development of the country. The fear of politicians may be that there would have been too much pain and this would have resulted

---

[59] Wikipedia, the online encyclopedia

in the loss of state power. The closed economy of the 1980s resulted in a productive sector that was not used to dealing with competition and the high interest rates of the 1990s did little to encourage the transition. Higher interest rates ultimately resulted in much needed macroeconomic stability but set the ball rolling on what would become a significant debt trap because of the productivity issues.

The liberalization of the exchange and import controls, in the 1990s, was too sudden for an economy that has always practiced protectionism, where the local players, who have been protected from global competition for so long, were not ready for the inevitable global onslaught. The result was that the rate of exchange depreciated from US$1.00:J$6.50 on January 1, 1990 to US$1.00:J$40.01 on January 2, 1996. This in turn drove inflation to as high as 80.2 percent in 1991.

The relationship between debt, GDP, the exchange rate, and inflation was not restricted to the 1990s only. The same problem with Jamaica occurred during the 1980s, as in order to keep a stable exchange rate there was a trade off with relatively high inflation and a climbing debt/GDP ratio, when in 1984 the debt/GDP ratio peaked at 212 percent. Even during the latter half of the 1980s, when growth of over six percent was being experienced, the exchange rate depreciated by over 48 percent between 1986 and 1990, moving from US$1.00:J$5.50 to US$1.00:J$8.17, and the inflation rate averaged 17 percent per annum[60] for those five years.

Chart 9 gives a graphical representation of the debt/GDP ratio, inflation, and exchange rate movement between 1980 and 2007. It shows clearly that the policies pursued to stabilize one or more indicators led to a trade off with the worsening of the others. The reason for this is because as mentioned in chapters 4 and 5, the economy is not properly structured to

---

[60] WER

benefit from growth, and the focus of government policy has always been on managing the symptoms (inflation, exchange rate, and debt/GDP ratio) rather than the underlying problems of productivity and the production and social relationships. The reason for this however has to do with, in my view, the lack of political will, as the pursuit of the appropriate fiscal policies would have been detrimental to holding on to state power.

Chart 9: Debt/GDP, Inflation, and Rate of Exchange 1980 to 2007 (Source: BOJ and WER)[1]

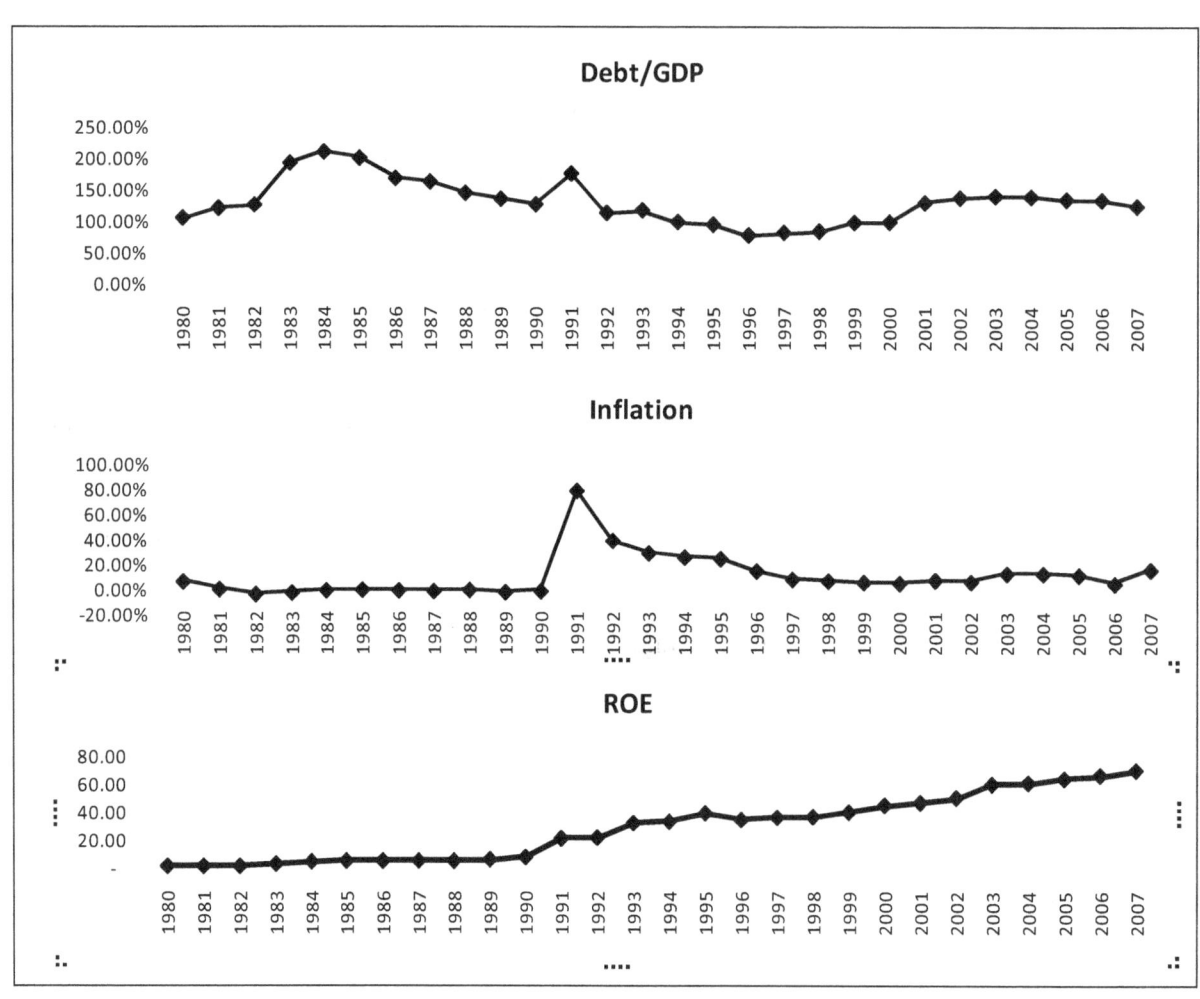

1980s: the focus was on keeping the exchange rate stable by using a managed exchange rate system. This resulted in a thriving black market and very high debt/GDP ratios and high inflation despite relatively high growth rates.

1990s: the focus was on keeping inflation low and managing down the debt/GDP ratio, but this resulted in a rapid devaluation of the Jamaican dollar versus the United States dollar.

2000s: the focus was on stabilizing the exchange rate, in an effort to manage inflation. This resulted in an increase in the debt/GDP ratio. During this period the economy was helped by record inflows of FDI.

There is a fundamental role for government to play, which is to (i) provide infrastructure and services that the market will not; (ii) protect the less fortunate; (iii) a regulatory role to promote law, order and discipline; and (iv) protect against erratic economic swings and implement policies to support development. In other words economies and countries work best when government provides a supporting role for the market, the leading actor. It is to promote this role to which economic and social policies should be directed. In relation to the people it does not mean providing them with handouts, or redistributing income, as Jamaica has always done, but rather providing the access to opportunities for the people to excel in their chosen endeavours.

Some of these policy initiatives should include:

✓ Access to a quality education right through to tertiary level – this can come in the form of free education to secondary level and scholarships and loans to the tertiary level. It is important for government to play the lead role in educating the masses. Allocation of resources to this will have very positive long term effects.

✓ Access to quality health care, which should be a cost borne mostly by the state, as productivity can only be based on a healthy population. The Human Development Report reveals that the top ten ranked countries, for HDI[61], spend an average of 7 percent of GDP on health and 5.9 percent on education. The average GDP per capita for these top ten countries is US$34,413. Similarly, the 17 regional countries listed in Table 22, spent an average of 3.6 percent and 5.9 percent of GDP on health and education respectively, with an average GDP per capita of US$9,017. The implication is that higher health care spending, and access, could result in a healthier population that may serve to improve productivity and also allow for greater impact of education, as a healthier person would not only attend school more regularly but be able to absorb more from education. One of the difficulties regional countries faces, when compared to the high income countries, is that a relatively high amount of GDP is spent on debt servicing. So while debt may have a short term benefit for macroeconomic stability, and political objectives, if not used properly for long term development it can have a deleterious effect on long term economic and social development.

✓ Tax policy geared towards human development - Table 24, on page 99, shows the ranking of the 2007/08 HDI ranking[62]. The table also shows the 2005 tax as a percentage of GDP[63] from data compiled by EUROSTAT and the OECD.

---

[61] Human Development Report Table 19

[62] Human Development Report 2007/08

[63] www.wikipedia.com

Table 23: Priority Expenditure (Source: Human Development Report 2007/08)

HDI Rank	Public expenditure on health (% of GDP) 2004	Public expenditure on education (% of GDP)		Military expenditure (% of GDP)		Total debt service (% of GDP)	
		1991	2002-05	1990	2005	1990	2005
31 Barbados	4.5	7.8	6.9	0.8	0.8	8.2	3.1
48 Costa Rica	5.1	3.4	4.9	0.0	0.0	6.8	3.0
49 Bahamas	3.4	3.7	3.6	0.8	0.7	..	..
51 Cuba	5.5	9.7	9.8	..	..	..	..
54 Saint Kitts & Nevis	3.3	2.7	9.3	..	..	1.9	10.6
57 Antigua & Barbuda	3.4	..	3.8	..	..	..	..
59 Trinidad & Tobago	1.4	4.1	4.2	..	..	8.9	2.6
71 Dominica	4.2	..	5.0	..	..	3.5	6.0
72 Saint Lucia	3.3	..	5.8	..	..	1.6	4.0
79 Dominican Republic	1.9	..	1.8	0.6	0.5	3.3	3.0
80 Belize	2.7	4.6	5.4	1.2	..	4.4	20.7
82 Grenada	5.0	4.9	5.2	..	..	1.5	2.6
85 Suriname	3.6	5.9	..	..	..	..	..
93 Saint Vincent & the Grenadines	3.9	5.9	8.2	..	..	2.2	5.5
97 Guyana	4.4	2.2	8.5	0.9	..	74.5	4.2
101 Jamaica	2.8	4.5	5.3	0.6	0.6	14.4	10.1
146 Haiti	2.9	1.4	..	..	..	1.3	1.4

The column to the right of the HDI ranking shows 2005 tax as a percentage of GDP. Although the top ten countries in the HDI ranking shows higher tax as a percentage of GDP, it clearly implies a higher relation between tax revenues and the development of human capital. In the case of Jamaica tax revenues go primarily to meet debt servicing costs. For countries ranked in the tax range of Jamaica, the United States, South Korea, and Romania, their HDI rankings were 12, 26, and 60 respectively, while Jamaica ranked at 101. It is important to note also that Romania was previously a communist state. From a social development point of view it is therefore very important to ensure that tax revenues are directed at human development policies.

Table 24: Human Development Index Ranking and Tax as
% of GDP[64]

Country	HDI Ranking	Tax as % of GDP
Iceland	1	42.4%
Norway	2	44.3%
Australia	3	30.9%
Canada	4	33.4%
Ireland	5	30.8%
Sweden	6	51.3%
Switzerland	7	29.7%
Japan	8	38.2%
Netherlands	9	44.0%
France	10	27.3%
United States	12	25.5%
South Korea	26	N/A
Barbados	31	N/A
Bahamas	49	N/A
Cuba	51	N/A
Saint Kitts & Nevis	54	N/A
Antigua & Barbuda	57	N/A
Trinidad & Tobago	59	N/A
Romania	60	27.4%
Dominica	71	N/A
Saint Lucia	72	N/A
Grenada	82	N/A
Suriname	85	N/A
Saint Vincent & the Grenadines	93	N/A
Guyana	97	N/A
Jamaica	101	25.9%
Haiti	146	N/A

✓ Efficient and equitable justice system – this means an efficient court system, modern legislation, and a corrupt free and efficient security force. People, and companies, whose rights have been abused, must be able to get proper legal representation and swift action from the courts. As an example, the failure to get

---

[64] Sources: UNDP 2007/08 Human development Report and Wikipedia, the online encyclopedia

commercial transactions resolved in the courts swiftly can affect business transactions and thereby hamper economic activity, which can lead to an inefficient market.

✓ Efficient public sector, that is not mired in bureaucracy and inefficiency, as has been the case with Jamaica's civil service at least since the 1990s. The public sector is nothing more than the implementation arm of government policies and if it remains as inefficient as it has been then the policies aimed at development will not be effectively implemented to bring about change. Therefore productivity and efficiency must be encouraged in the public sector or else even if the correct policy initiatives are in place they will not be effectively implemented.

This was the problem with the Public Sector Memorandum of Understanding (MOU) introduced in 2004. Based on the wording of the MOU it was obvious that, although it said so, it could never achieve economic development, and was going to make the economic challenges even more difficult. The MOU was nothing more than a wage agreement designed to give the government some fiscal breathing space, and made a fundamental error, in that it sought to reward everyone in the same way irrespective of productivity. The MOU was never geared towards improved efficiency in the public sector and correctly so never mentioned productivity.

In a speech to the Rotary Club of Spanish Town on February 17, 2004, I espoused the importance of the proposed Partnership for Progress. I also cautioned against the implementation of the MOU because of the same productivity concern. History has proven that the MOU has not helped and in fact has made the economic challenges even more difficult as Jamaica still has an inefficient public sector and each year faces the possibility of industrial action because of difficulty in agreeing the MOU.

If the necessary changes are to be made to economic and social policy, public sector reform is not only extremely important but necessary.

Chart 10: Economic and Social Development Building Blocks

Chart 10 is a simple illustration of what is required for real economic and social development. It puts forward the argument that while it is recognized that the efficient organization and allocation of the factors of production are necessary for maximizing productivity and achieving economic growth, this is not sufficient for economic and social development. And while from the discussion in chapter 4, it is determined that economic growth does not guarantee economic development, similarly economic development does not guarantee social development.

It is necessary for the economy to be structured towards exports if we are truly to achieve sustainable economic development. But sustainable economic development alone will not result in social development, because it is possible to have economic development without social development. In other words while an economy may grow by ten percent or more this does not guarantee that most of the population will still not be mired in poverty. A country's development should therefore not only focus on economics but must also strive for social development[65].

One fundamental flaw of most introductory economic text books on the market economy is that while it explains the theory behind the workings of the market economy it makes certain assumptions about the environment. The assumption is made of a market where information is freely shared and demand and supply reacts to relative prices, rather than any external forces. Introductory economic theory also inherently assumes that the political and governance system is one that will allow for the proper workings of the market. In other words it assumes that public policy is supportive of market development. This is the main reason why to the layman the market economy does not seem to work in a country like Jamaica. Someone schooled in economics may understand the fundamental role of public policy in the efficiency of markets but the problem is that most policy makers are not so trained and so do not understand the vital link between public policy and economic and social development. The result is that it leads to arguments for and against both capitalism and socialism.

This is the fundamental division between the proponents of capitalism and socialism. On the one hand capitalism has proved to be the best system for achieving economic growth

---

[65] Jamaica has not had the correct mix, as during the 1970s the focus was on social development to the detriment of economic development and in the 1980s to present the focus has been on economic development to the detriment of social development.

and development but socialists argue it does not sufficiently address the need for social equality. Even in the symbol of capitalism - the United States - there are still pockets of severe poverty despite its economic achievements. The 2008 financial crisis in the United States has encouraged some to argue against capitalism in favour of a socialist state. Whatever the arguments are, no one can deny that capitalism has been the best system for economic development and therefore the compromise must be for a capitalist system with government providing regulatory and social support to protect the weak and provide opportunities for all[66]. In other words the way of the future must be a hybrid system that brings about both economic and social development[67].

As was discussed earlier, Chart 10 illustrates that in order for quality economic growth to take place, Jamaica needs to implement positive public policy, through fiscal policies and incentives, and a properly and equitably organized social opportunity system. This inevitably includes the need for an efficient and less bureaucratic public sector system that is geared towards supporting an efficient market economy.

From a practical perspective, however, before any such public policy system can be put in place it is necessary to have a political structure that naturally allows the checks and balances for the implementation and continuation of progressive public policy.

IV. **A New Political Structure**: This brings us to what I believe to be the fundamental driver of an efficient market economy and the key to either (i) economic development; (ii) social development; or (iii) economic and social development.

---

[66] Is capitalism dead? ; Dennis Chung; Jamaica Observer, October 17, 2008 and dcjottings.blogspot.com

[67] In the wake of the 2008 financial crisis, government's role must be increased as it is only through government intervention in leading projects that the markets will recover in an acceptable time frame.

I say either one of these three outcomes because at one extreme - laissez faire capitalism - there could be significant economic development at the expense of social stability, as it would see extreme poverty for most while a minority would enjoy extreme wealth. This would no doubt ultimately result in social unrest as the basic instinct of human beings is to survive at all costs and under a laissez faire system there are no regulations to control crime or excesses under capitalism as it is not profitable to do so and the service would therefore not be provided. The 2007/08 financial crisis in the United States is an example of what can happen in the absence of regulations in the financial markets, as companies wrote mortgages without proper risk management ultimately resulting in the collapse of the global financial system. One of the primary causes of this was the lack of proper regulatory oversight of the financial markets as a result of too much deregulation.

At the other end, extreme socialism, or communism as defined by Marx and Engel, there would be social equality for all and there would be no class distinction. The problem with communism or Marxism, as it is known, is that the market ceases to operate efficiently as the state takes full control of the distribution of resources. Sooner or later inefficiency and corruption will creep into the system and economic stagnation will result, which inevitably impoverishes the country. The experience of probably the two most famous communist states, the USSR and China, are examples that extreme communism will not work as it ultimately leads to increased poverty for most of the people and underdevelopment of the country. China with all its celebrated growth rates only accounts for approximately six percent of world's output, while the United States commands 25 percent.

It is obvious therefore that the best political system is a hybrid of both capitalism and communism, such as we find in places like Switzerland. There is no direct relationship between a political system and economic growth or development, as this not only has to do with the political system but also the literacy levels and other resources. But what is clear is that the political system is important in achieving the literacy and maximizing the resources that lead to economic development.

If one looks at the top ten countries in terms of per capita GDP ranking in 2007[68], it includes only one country with some form of variant of a Westminster system, which is Ireland ranked at number seven. Everyone in Jamaica should by now know the Ireland success story as it has been a topic of intense study. The difference between Ireland and Jamaica is that, despite having a variant of the Westminster model, they managed to get a power sharing agreement between the two opposing parties and so the focus is on development rather than political power. Ireland also has a literacy rate of close to 100 percent, while Jamaica's is approximately 80 percent. Of the other countries in the top ten they have either monarchies, parliamentary democracies, or a republican type system. Three of these (Qatar, Brunei, and Kuwait) are oil producing countries and oil rose to record prices between 2007 and 2008.

What is more important, however, and emphasizes the need for a system that promotes social development also, is that of the top ten countries, the United States is number six but is also the most sought after country for immigrants. This may be because it not only has good economic development but also acceptable social development. So that the mixture between economic and social development in the United States makes it probably the most sought after place of residence for many. The United States is ranked twelfth in the 2007/08 HDI ranking and in 2005 showed tax as a percentage of GDP at a relatively low 27.3 percent for similar HDI rankings. The United States is a constitutional republic with separation of powers. Under the constitutional republic *"...the executive, legislative, and judicial powers are separated into distinct branches and the will of the majority of the*

---

[68] Wikipedia, the online encyclopedia

population is tempered by protections for individual rights so that no individual or group has absolute power "[69]

Jamaica practices a Westminster system modelled on the United Kingdom Westminster system, and is ranked 87th in terms of per capita GDP. The other countries with a variant of the Westminster model are Antigua and Barbuda, Bahamas, Barbados, Belize, Dominica, Grenada, Saint Kitts and Nevis, Saint Lucia, Saint Vincent and the Grenadines, and Trinidad and Tobago. The highest ranked country is Bahamas, at 33.

My own view is that while the Westminster system of government works for the United Kingdom it is unsuitable for small states like Jamaica, especially as it is practiced. I will try to justify this by briefly looking at the Westminster system as practiced in the United Kingdom in comparison to Jamaica.

In the United Kingdom the system of governance includes at the head the monarchy, or head of state - currently the Queen. The United Kingdom holds elections every five years, and elects 650 members of parliament, one representing each constituency. These 650 members constitute the Parliament, which is the supreme political body in the country, as it consists of members who all were elected by the people and are deemed to represent the people. This is the Westminster system's way of giving power of governance to the people. The Queen then selects a Prime Minister from the political party that has won the most constituencies. The Prime Minister is then invited by the Queen to form the government by selecting ministers of government primarily from the elected members of parliament. There are three major political parties in the United Kingdom, namely Conservatives, Labour Party, and Liberal Democrats. There is also the Scottish National Party that is represented in parliament.

---

[69] Wikipedia, the online encyclopedia

In Jamaica, the head of state is represented by the Governor General, and is largely ceremonial as is the situation with the monarchy in the United Kingdom. Similarly the Governor General appoints the Prime Minister from the party that has won the majority, from the two political parties, the JLP and the PNP. Elections are constitutionally due every five years from the date of the last election, but can be called at any time during the five years by the Prime Minister. The political geography consists of 60 constituencies.

The difference between the United Kingdom and Jamaica can be seen as follows:

➢ The United Kingdom has 650 members of parliament from which there are usually 20 senior government ministers and maybe about 100 members of parliament forming the government. So that even if a party has a majority number of seats of 326, approximately one-third would form the government, and there would be another 324 members in opposition. The total number of persons that form government is therefore approximately one sixth of the parliament. In Jamaica's case anywhere between 15 and 20 will be senior government ministers, and there are another 13 senators appointed by the Governor General on the advice of the Prime Minister. So from a 31 seat majority one could see all 31 appointed as either ministers of government or senators. The result is that whereas in the United Kingdom there are checks and balances on the government by the non government members of parliament, there is little if any in Jamaica.

What makes this even more pronounced is that the leader of the political party, who usually ends up being Prime Minister, will appoint the constituency caretakers who will run for members of parliament in the elections.

➢ In the United Kingdom, the head of state is not appointed but comes from a bloodline, being the first born of the reigning monarch on his/her death. So that there is no political interference in the appointment of the head of state, who has the right to dissolve parliament, as in Jamaica. The problem in Jamaica is that the resident head of state, the Governor General, who theoretically has significant powers under the constitution, is appointed by the monarch in the United Kingdom effectively on the recommendation of the Jamaican Prime Minister. Once that appointment is done the Queen/King will not seek to interfere to remove that appointment irrespective of how ineffective the Governor General is. The result is that the control of the Governor General really rests with the Prime Minister.

➢ Further when one examines the Jamaican constitution; it shows that the appointments of government ministers, the Attorney General, Director of Public Prosecutions, and Police Services Commission (who appoints the Police Commissioner) are made by the Governor General *"in accordance with the recommendation of the Prime Minister"*.

So in Jamaica we have a political system where for all practical purposes absolute power rests with the Prime Minister, unlike in a constitutional republic, and there are no real checks and balance on his/her power. This has resulted in a situation where the appointed ministers, police force, prosecutors, and by extension the boards of government bodies are effectively at the mercy of the Prime Minister.

This absolute type of power leads to is a fight for state power at all costs. So as has been the case in Jamaica since 1962, when the governing party is faced with a choice between state power or economic and social development, state power will more than likely always be the choice. In the case of Trinidad and Barbados they have had two Prime Ministers, Chambers and Sandiford respectively, who were willing to sacrifice their political careers for the good of the country. Both countries did benefit but they lost state power.

My own view is that a constitutional republican system, as practiced in the United States, is best suited for small states like Jamaica, in conjunction with a market economy and a government that ensures equal opportunity, justice, and protects from the excesses of capitalism within the framework of that market economy. While it is possible to have a Prime Minister interested in the country's development, such as Sandiford, this is not a guarantee. We also must accept that it is the primary role of political parties to seek state power and so whatever they can do, within the confines of the law and morality, to gain state power is acceptable and should be expected. This is why a political system that will ensure that decisions do not go against what is good for the country is necessary.

Until Jamaica can reform its political system so that the necessary checks and balances are in place, and the elected representatives, the police, and the Governor General are truly independent then we may possibly achieve some economic growth but not necessarily the quality that will lead to economic and social development.

V. **The Role of Civil Society**: Even though Government is responsible for the general direction of the country, there is a fundamental role for civil society to play. Democracy we must remember is defined as *"government by the people for the people"*. This means that the people should always be vigilant in ensuring that the elected representatives[70] carry out their wishes. And this is very possible in Jamaica also, as politicians do on most occasions yield to public pressure. For example the 1999 gas riots saw the then government bowing to the will of the people and rolling back the gas tax that was imposed. This is driven by the desire to retain state power, which is the role of political parties.

---

[70] The 60 members of parliament in Jamaica

A big part of the problem Jamaica has faced, however, is that civil society has not sufficiently provided the necessary checks and balances for reasons including the following:

- o As a result of the state tentacles being so much involved in the economy, without the appropriate checks and balances, many private sector leaders are unwilling to speak out against the state;

- o Many private sector leaders are aligned to one political party or another, just like the average Jamaican. They are therefore not willing to call it as they see it for fear of losing business if their party is not in power; and

- o One could argue that many Jamaicans do not properly understand the economic and social policies needed to drive the country's development because the main concern of many Jamaicans is basic survival and so short term gain is more rewarding than any thought of long term development.

VI. **Summary**: There is an inextricable link between the political structure and economic and social development, as illustrated by Chart 10. While economic development is desirable and necessary, it does not guarantee total development of a country. Total development includes not only economic development but also social development. Jamaica has had neither relative economic nor social development, in comparison to other regional countries, and has only implemented economic policies in order to stabilize the economic variables of inflation and the exchange rate.

The main thing that has been lacking in the quest for the implementation of policies, to support sustainable economic and social development, is the political will; as such policies could probably result in a loss of state power. The current Westminster system practiced by

Jamaica does not facilitate the checks and balances needed for government and the opposition to act truly in the interest of the people.

As a result of the economic and other challenges being faced by many Jamaicans, civil society also has not provided the role it should in a thriving democracy. This, it can be argued, is because of the high involvement of the state in directing economic resources and the fact that many Jamaicans do not understand what is required for true long term development.

The probability is that before Jamaica can truly achieve economic and social development it may need to define a new political and social order.

Chapter 8: CONCLUSION- A MODEL FOR ECONOMIC AND SOCIAL DEVELOPMENT

The analysis in prior chapters, using what I have referred to as "Accountonomics", illustrates that Jamaica's economy is not structured for economic and social development. In the first instance Jamaica is not structured for economic development because its main growth areas are net users of foreign exchange and therefore place significant pressures on the Balance of Payments. The result is that whenever Jamaica achieves economic growth it is going to be always worse for the long term prospects of the economy under the present production relationships.

The short answer is that Jamaica has primarily a Balance of Payments challenge, which in turn causes a foreign exchange shortage, which results in (i) depreciation pressure on the Jamaican dollar; (ii) relatively high inflation; (iii) deterioration of real income and social challenges; (iv) the need for greater debt; and (v) a fiscal challenge. The Balance of Payments challenge is itself caused by Jamaica's production and productivity relationships that result in a greater consumption of imports than what is exported. This production and productivity challenge results primarily from Jamaica's political structure.

Unless Jamaica changes this set of production relationships then it will never be able to dig itself out of the economic stagnation it has faced since the end of the 1960s. Even the high growth rates experienced during the latter part of the 1980s had its negative consequences in terms of high inflation rates, and this caused a build up in inflationary pressures, which was partially responsible for the devaluations in the 1990s. The main reason for the official exchange rate being stable in the 1980s was because of exchange control but there was at the time a thriving "black" market[71].

In order for Jamaica to turn the corner and start on the path to economic and social development it requires the following:

> A fundamental shift in its production relationships towards export and productivity – this means a redefinition of the economic model;

> A redefinition of the political and social order; and

> A real shift to a market economy supported by government in the role of facilitator of economic support and equal opportunity.

This definition of a new economic, social, and political order requires first that Jamaica examine the appropriateness of the Westminster system as its political structure, as in its present form it has been an inhibitor rather than a facilitator of economic and social development. Real economic and social development can only result from the initiatives of fiscal policies by the government. So the first step to achieving the goal of much needed economic and social development is to ensure that government policies are aligned with developmental goals. The objective of any political party, whether in government or not, should be to secure state power but what is needed is a political structure that will allow for the necessary checks and balances to ensure the interests of the people and country are represented first and foremost. A system such as a constitutional republic that provides for separation of powers may be more appropriate for Jamaica's development.

---

[71] Unofficial secondary market where the United States dollar was being traded at rates significantly in excess of the official "controlled" exchange rate. So even while the exchange rate was managed, the market forces created a secondary market that was more in line with the demand and supply for United States dollars.

Even if the appropriate political structure is in place, that will ensure policy initiatives geared towards economic and social development, this is still not enough. These policies require an efficient mechanism for their implementation. The present public sector has proven to be bureaucratic and inefficient, and therefore cannot effectively implement the necessary initiatives. The 2004 MOU further entrenched the inefficiencies of the public sector by guaranteeing that everyone is given the same reward irrespective of productivity levels. That combined with a system of job tenure means that there is no incentive to strive for efficiency.

Therefore Jamaica must tackle the problem of public sector efficiency and bureaucracy so that it does not stand in the way of the market operating efficiently. Efficient public sector reform must be one of the highest priorities. The public policies that need to be implemented must include better quality education and health access, a significantly improved justice system, and better social support for the unemployed. Government policy must also create incentives for export led growth[72], as the market will most certainly need a jump start to allocate resources to the export led areas.

Fiscal policy can be a significant determinant in the efficient allocation of resources and is required if Jamaica is to break out of the vicious cycle of increasing debt, inflation, and exchange rate, while experiencing economic and social stagnation. The past policies of allocating resources to failing industries such as sugar have only served to hasten Jamaica's economic stagnation.

The achievement of an economic and social structure can only be achieved by starting with the base on the building blocks in Chart 10. A failure to make that fundamental shift will

---

[72] Export led growth can be defined as meaning sectors that earn or save foreign exchange for the country. So tourism and agriculture for import substitution would qualify.

ensure that Jamaica does not begin to see the necessary changes needed for economic and social development.

Chart 11 summarizes the both the current model and the needed paradigm shift for the economy. The chart to the left represents the current economic structure and the chart on the right the paradigm shift if the mentioned fiscal policies are implemented. The difference between both charts is that the current economic model lacks foreign exchange in the system and the new paradigm has a surplus of foreign exchange.

The implication is that fiscal policies must be geared towards activities/initiatives that will either (i) improve foreign exchange earnings, (ii) decrease foreign exchange expenditure, or (iii) a combination of both. This is something that monetary policy cannot achieve so that policies of interest rate manipulation or higher borrowing will not fix the long term economy, and is primarily the reason why Jamaica's economy is in the position it is today. What monetary policy can do is affect the flow of foreign exchange but not the earning potential.

The only way to achieve long term foreign currency surplus is for Jamaica to be a net earner from international trade. This implies increasing production and productivity in export oriented sectors, which means changing the relationship between export and non-export sectors in total GDP output. What Jamaica has been doing, especially since the 1990s, to close this foreign exchange gap is to borrow money. This has its own consequences as no person, or country, will be able to borrow money continuously without reaching its credit limit, and in getting to that credit limit incurring increasing borrowing costs. Along that path the disposable income for spending on one's self also declines, assuming that you honour your debts, and if you don't then that has other consequences.

The only true way for Jamaica to earn more than it spends is to shift from the current production relationships to a new paradigm.

Chart 11: Current Economic Model and Paradigm Shift of Micro and Macro Economy

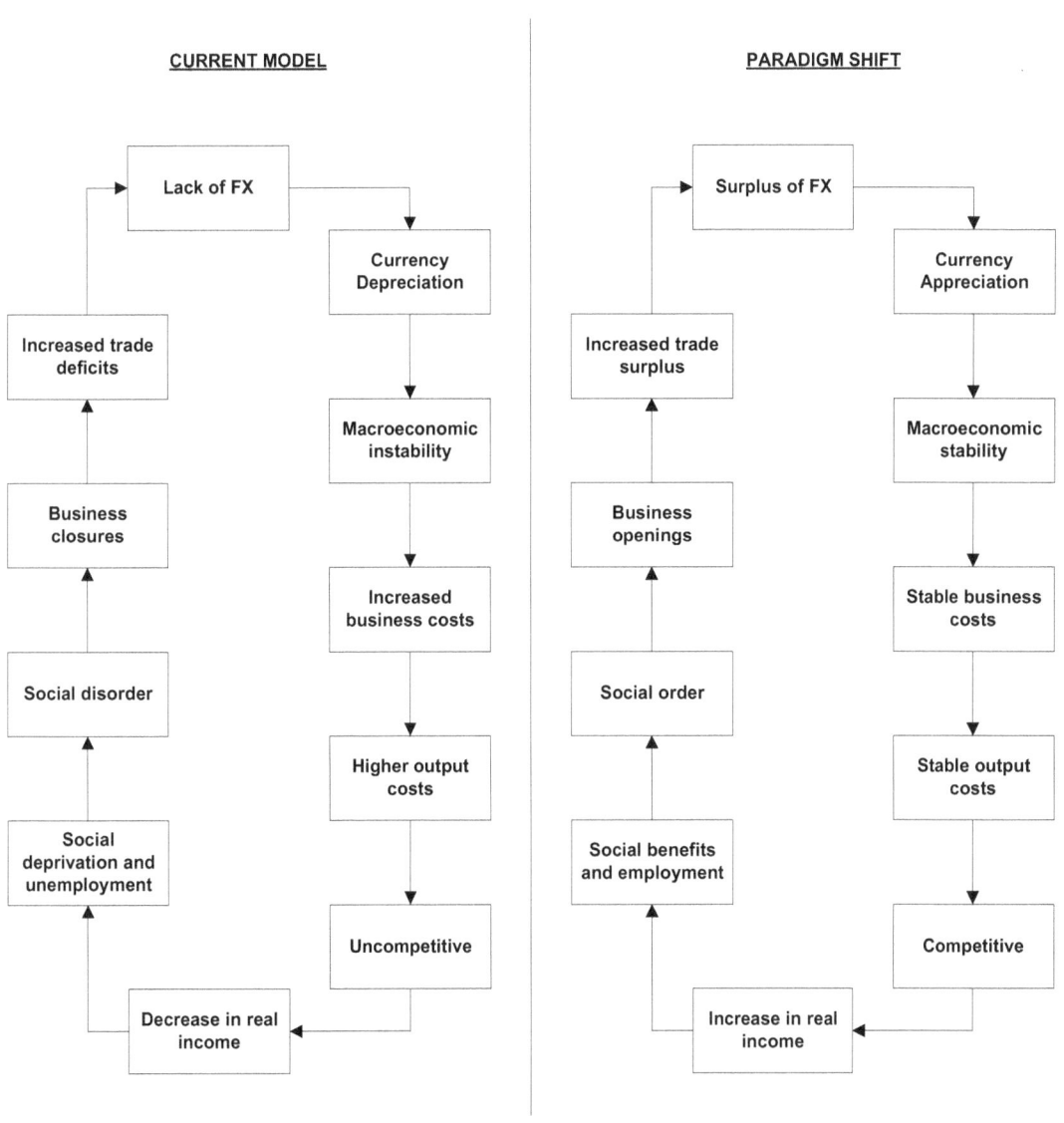

This implies that government must pursue fiscal policies to encourage production and allow the private sector to become the dominant player in the market rather than the bureaucracy of the public sector and the use of monetary policy. In order for the market to work effectively however, equal opportunity (a level playing field) and justice must prevail,

---

Changing Jamaica's production relationships to create a paradigm shift

Chart 11 compares the current economic structure to a new paradigm if deliberate fiscal policies are introduced to encourage the increase of export earning sectors in GDP total output. This will have the impact of increasing the net foreign exchange earnings for Jamaica. The explanation of both models are as follows:

Current Economic Structure:

Jamaica imports significantly more than it exports and this causes a lack of foreign exchange needed to satisfy Jamaica's appetite for imports. This results because Jamaica's economic structure is geared towards output for local consumption rather than export. This shortage of foreign exchange results in currency depreciation, which in turn threatens macroeconomic stability. This leads to increased business costs, resulting in higher output costs (inflation). The result is uncompetitiveness, a decrease in real incomes, increased unemployment. Lower fiscal revenues, from lower profits, combined with higher unemployment will no doubt lead to social disorder, as resources are unavailable for preventing this, such as through security or a social safety net. This will eventually lead to business closures and increased trade deficits starting the downward spiralling circle.

In order to slow the downward trend Jamaica has used monetary policies and increased borrowings as tools. But at best these tools offer only short term solutions.

Paradigm Shift (strategic fiscal policies introduced):

By introducing fiscal policies aimed at improving the mix of exports as a percentage of total GDP output, Jamaica can improve its net foreign exchange position. If this is done effectively enough to create a foreign exchange surplus in the system then this will have the effect of creating an appreciation of the Jamaican dollar. This will in turn create macroeconomic stability resulting in a stable and predictive business environment and stable output costs (inflation). Competitiveness will increase translating into higher real incomes, employment, and training as new skills will be needed. The GoJ will earn greater fiscal revenues as profits increase, without having to raise taxes, and will be able to provide greater social benefits and more resources for social order. New businesses will open in this environment, as equity and debt becomes more available, which will result in trade surpluses.

The country will develop both economically and socially as illustrated. At some point the central bank will have to step in with monetary policy to control inflation from an overheating economy but this will only slow the rate of development not stop economic and social development.

Note that it is only the introduction of a foreign exchange surplus in the equation that changes the output. Therefore the fiscal policies that should be pursued must be aimed at increasing foreign exchange net earnings for Jamaica.

else the system will spiral into disorder and without a predictable structure, businesses and the market -as promoted by economic theory - cannot work effectively. In order to ensure that equal opportunity, justice, and good governance prevails, implies a political structure that includes the necessary checks and balances to ensure that government finds it difficult to force a decision in the interest of state power in preference economic and social development.

The global financial crisis (2007/08) has added to the debate of what hybrid of capitalism and socialism is best for the long term sustainable development of a country. Jamaica no doubt needs to examine this and decide on the best model for its own development, as the Westminster model in my view is not suited for Jamaica's economic and social development. When we are speaking about economic development and the way markets operate it is important to consider the political structure.

The development and implementation of these policy initiatives while remaining the ultimate responsibility of government must involve the participation of all stakeholders to increase the probability of success. This of course does not mean that government will divest itself of the responsibility and authority to do what they have been elected to do, govern in the best interest of the people of Jamaica. There should however be a defined time period for consultation with all stakeholders, not least of which are civil society and the multi-laterals who should provide a greater portion of their support in the areas of technical assistance and education in Jamaica's development, particularly at the community level.

EPILOGUE: *Understanding Jamaica's currency challenge*

Jamaica has for a very long time had a currency challenge. Up until January 12, 1978, Jamaica's currency was valued at more than the United States dollar when the rate of exchange was US$1:J$0.91. Ever since then Jamaica's currency has been on a downward slide against the United States dollar. The year 1978 and before is not a period that most Jamaicans today remember clearly and many would only remember the struggle successive governments have had trying to reign in the depreciation of the Jamaican dollar versus the United States dollar.

Chart 12: Jamaica's Exchange Rate Movement (1971 to 2009) - Source: BOJ website

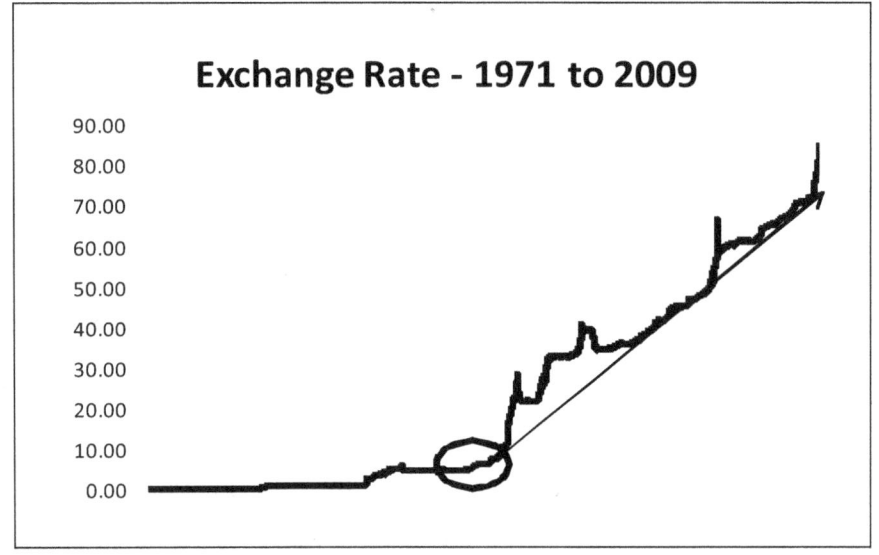

The chart shows the movement in the exchange rate between the Jamaican and United States dollars.

Since 1990 to 1991 we see where the Jamaican dollar has been on a steady downward trend against the United States dollar, which can be illustrated by drawing a trend line connecting the bottom points of the graph.

This consistent depreciation in the exchange rate has, and continues to cause havoc for the Jamaican people, as it has resulted in either one of two results – (i) high interest rates; or (ii) high inflation. Either one has proven detrimental for the Jamaican people. The high interest rate policy pursued in the 1990s to stabilize the exchange rate resulted in the collapse of many businesses ultimately leading to the failure of the whole financial system. High interest rates have led to the steep erosion of disposable income levels.

Because of the effect of devaluations on the Jamaican people, politicians have always pursued policies that seek to stabilize the exchange rate. There are basically three situations that can cause a stabilization of the exchange rate, which can be identified as follows:

1. Printing Jamaican currency – this creates a short term perception of wealth as it creates more Jamaican dollars in the economy, which means people and businesses will have more Jamaican dollars to spend. But then when it comes time to replace the imported goods in the economy, against the background of the increased demand created by the printed money, we find that there is more Jamaican dollars chasing the same supply of United States dollar. This ultimately causes the depreciation of the exchange rate, as what is created is monetary inflation. This policy was pursued in the 1970s mainly.

2. Borrowing foreign currency – this would be the policy that most Jamaicans have become accustomed to as it has been the weapon of choice against exchange rate depreciation since the 1980s, when the debt/GDP ratio reached a high of 212 percent. This causes a greater supply of foreign currency to come in the system, and as long as sufficient money can be borrowed results in macroeconomic stability. The problem with this policy is that if GDP cannot grow at a faster pace than the debt then the country will end up using most of its money for debt servicing, and will find it difficult to provide money for social and capital spending within the country. This ultimately will result in debt default and the impoverishment of the country. Today Jamaica uses 56 percent of its fiscal budget to service debt, and this has resulted in a lack of funding for social and infrastructural spending.

3. Export more than we import - the final option is to export more United States dollar value than we import. This is the only policy option that can lead to sustained stability and eventual appreciation of the Jamaican dollar. The only way for this to happen is not just by growing GDP, but rather by increasing exports until they surpass imports. It is these policy options that this book has been recommending and has been outlined in the Appendix.

Unless Jamaica can implement policy actions that eventually result in the country earning more foreign currency than it spends then the only two other measures available to the country will be options 1 or 2, and both have long term negative consequences. Earning more foreign exchange than what is spent does not only mean growing exports, but can also result by contracting imports.

So as an example in the 1980s the Seaga led government of the time restricted motor vehicle imports and when travelling one was only allowed to carry up to US$50 per trip. This of course did not help as it created a "black market"[73] for the United States dollar, and while the official exchange rate was at US$1:J$5.50 unofficially the real rate of exchange was significantly above that, so that we were living in a false sense of stability[74]. It is for this reason why I have consistently maintained that a managed, pegged, or fixed exchange rate cannot work effectively for the medium to long term.

One could also, however, produce goods and services locally that will replace imports. This of course will cause a lower demand for foreign exchange and is one area of opportunity, especially in the area of agriculture. On the side of services Jamaicans can also be encouraged to take more vacations within the country, as opposed to going overseas and carrying foreign currency out of the country.

Whether one exports more or produces more locally to replace imports, the result is the same – the only way to do this is by increasing production and productivity. It is only an increase in productivity that can make Jamaica's goods and services more competitive and result in them being preferred to foreign goods and services. It is to this core principle of improving production and productivity that policies must be aimed if we are to have true long term sustainable development.

The implementation of these policies of course can be painful and is therefore affected by the political system, as governments will always implement policies in order to retain state power. Over the years it has been easier to either print money or borrow foreign currency to give the impression of stability and progress so that elections are assured.

In the final analysis, however, it comes down to the Jamaican people who must demand that the right policies for long term development are in place. This renewal of thought can only come through a greater awareness and those who have the knowledge and understanding must make it their duty to impart this knowledge to the Jamaican people.

---

[73] Unofficial trading market

[74] Exchange control restrictions were necessary at the time (1980s) to facilitate economic restructuring and would be difficult today because of the greater dependency on the sentiments of the capital markets.

At December 2007 Jamaica's GDP value stood at US$7,847 million, at an assumed exchange rate of US$1:J$74. By classifying the sectors into foreign exchange earnings and non foreign exchange earnings, Table 25 shows where Jamaica's foreign exchange earning sectors makeup 27.76 percent of the GDP values while 72.24 percent is for local consumption.

Table 25: Jamaica 2007 GDP Values (Source: STATIN)

	Jamaica 2007 GDP values		
	JM$M	US$M	% of GDP
Foreign exchange earning sectors			
Agriculture, forestry and fishing	27,293.77	368.83	4.70%
Mining, quarrying and refining	19,913.27	269.10	3.43%
Manufacture	43,273.47	584.78	7.45%
Food, beverages and tobacco	24,030.46	324.74	4.14%
Other manufacturing	19,243.01	260.04	3.31%
Hotels and restaurants	27,432.80	370.71	4.72%
	161,186.78	2,178.20	27.76%
Non foreign exchange earning sectors			
Electricity, gas and wate	17,043.78	230.32	2.94%
Construction	44,230.16	597.70	7.62%
Wholesale & retail trade, Repairs & installation of machinery	96,159.85	1,299.46	16.56%
Transport, storage & communications	62,636.35	846.44	10.79%
Finance & insurance services	56,845.90	768.19	9.79%
Real estate renting & business activities	49,263.91	665.73	8.48%
Producers of government services	59,328.48	801.74	10.22%
Other services	33,998.09	459.43	5.85%
	419,506.52	5,669.01	72.24%
TOTAL GDP	580,693.30	7,847.21	100.00%
Surplus/(Deficit)	(258,319.74)	(3,490.81)	-44.48%

Table 25 shows further that the deficit between the foreign exchange earnings and non foreign exchange earnings sectors was US$3,491 million, or 44.48 percent of GDP. This creates a need for foreign exchange as GDP production requires 70 to 80 percent of imported inputs. If 100 percent of inputs were local then there would be nothing wrong with even no exports as it means that local inputs would be equal to consumption and there would be no need for foreign exchange, which means that there would be no need for external debt and the rate of exchange would not be important.

Because Jamaica imports 70 to 80 percent of its consumption then foreign exchange becomes a problem, which translates to a need for debt (because earnings are less than expenditure), and this in turn drives interest rates and inflation higher.

In order to change this and drive economic development Jamaica needs to (i) reduce its dependence on imports; and/or (ii) increase its foreign exchange earnings sectors to be greater than the non foreign exchange sectors.

Let us assume the following:
- Jamaica imports 80 percent for production input, and uses 20 percent local inputs;
- Producers mark up on average by ten percent; and
- The rate of exchange is US$1:J$74

Based on the 2007 GDP J$ values, the net foreign exchange earnings can be represented as shown in Table 26. It shows that if producers mark up by ten percent then the cost of the GDP values is approximately J$145 billion export and J$381.4 billion non-export. If we assume that 80 percent of total production is from imports then this amounts to J$421.1 billion, which require foreign exchange.

Table 26: Assumed GDP Inputs

	Export J$Bn	Non-export J$Bn	Total J$Bn	US$Bn
GDP Values	159.5	419.5		
Cost of GDP values	145.0	381.4		
Local inputs	29.0	76.3		
Import input	(116.0)	(305.1)	(421.1)	(5.7)
Export earnings	159.5		159.5	2.2
Net FX earnings				(3.5)

Assumptions:
1. Producer marks up goods by 10 percent
2. Local inputs account for 20 percent of GDP value
3. Imports account for 80 percent of GDP value
4. Assumed rate of exchange (ROE) = US$1:J$74

On the other hand if we assume that the total GDP output from the export sectors come by way of foreign exchange earnings (which is aggressive) then it means that just by the way Jamaica's GDP is structured there is a foreign exchange deficit of J$262 billion, or US$3.5 billion, as import content is J$421.1 billion while export earning is only J$159.5 billion. In order for the Jamaican economy to be able to deal with this foreign exchange shortage it must in turn borrow money, leading to the high debt level Jamaica faces. This in turn translates to high interest rates, as demand for foreign exchange and Government risk rises, resulting in a sliding Jamaican dollar and inflation. The ultimate effect is social deprivation.

The solution

To solve this foreign exchange dilemma requires a change in the GDP sector structure. This may mean, in the short run, reducing the non foreign exchange earnings as limited resources means that one unit of resource cannot be employed to two separate uses at the same time.

123

Table 27: Initiatives to Change the GDP Structure

	Year 1 US$M	Year 2 US$M	Year 3 US$M	Year 4 US$M	Year 5 US$M	Total US$M	Comments
REDUCE DEPENDENCE ON IMPORTS:							
1 Substitution of imported foods for locally produced agriculture	-	36.54	36.54	36.54	36.54	146.16	2007 Food imports as basis
2 Discourage certain luxury imports for 2 years	75.34	75.34	-	-	-	150.68	2007 Manufactured goods import as basis
3 Reduce dependence on oil	-	362.34	362.34	362.34	362.34	1,449.36	Can be done by implementing more efficient transportation, discouraging private transportation, and encouraging alternative energy sources. 60% of oil consumption is estimated as retail (assume 20% reduction starting year 2)
4 Increase substitution of local input	-	-	-	8.42	8.42	16.84	Conservatively assume substituting 2% odf current import content into cost of GDP values starting year 4
Benefits from reducing import dependence	75.34	474.22	398.88	407.30	407.30	1,763.04	
INCREASE IN NET FX EARNINGS:							
1 Reallocation of resources to produce with competitive advantage	18.44	18.44	18.44	18.44	18.44	92.20	Assume 5% earnings increase per annum if either resources move away from sugar and bananas to more productive crops or increase competitive advantage in sugar and banana
2 Fiscal policies such as tax breaks to encourage greater export earnings	43.56	43.56	43.56	43.56	43.56	217.80	Assume 2% increase on total FX earnings sectors
3 Productivity improvements in FX earnings sectors	217.82	217.82	217.82	217.82	217.82	1,089.10	Assume 10% increase on increase on total FX earnings sectors
4 Reduce GOJ involvement in economy	-	38.52	38.52	38.52	38.52	154.08	Assume 5% in year 1 and 15% thereafter from public sector restructuring
Benefits from increased FX earnings	279.82	318.34	318.34	318.34	318.34	1,553.18	
TOTAL BALANCE OF PAYMENTS BENEFIT	355.16	792.56	717.22	725.64	725.64	3,316.22	

Table 27 outlines eight general fiscal policy initiatives that Jamaica could take to improve its foreign exchange position with a view to sustainable economic development. The benefits can be seen to accrue from these initiatives as follows:

Initiatives	FX Benefits
REDUCE DEPENDENCE ON IMPORTS:	
1.1. Substitution of imported foods for locally produced agriculture – here it assumed that between Years 2 and 5 Jamaican can substitute 20 percent of the imported food values with locally produced foods	Year 2 – US$ 36.54M Year 3 – US$ 36.54M Year 4 – US$ 36.54M Year 5 – US$ 36.54M TOTAL – US$146.14M
1.2. Fiscal policies to discourage import of certain luxury items for two years e.g. luxury vehicles, furniture etc – assume ten percent reduction in manufactured goods import value for two years	Year 1 – US$ 75.34M Year 2 – US$ 75.34M TOTAL – US$150.68M
1.3. Reduce dependence on oil – improved and strategic public transport, alternative energy – assume 20 percent reduction in the 60 percent oil consumption in transportation and retail household consumption	Year 2 – US$ 362.34M Year 3 – US$ 362.34M Year 4 – US$ 362.34M Year 5 – US$ 362.34M TOTAL – US$1449.36M
1.4. Increase substation of local input for imports, e.g. art and craft, vacation for Jamaicans etc. – assume two percent impact in years 4 and 5	Year 4 – US$ 8.42M Year 5 – US$ 8.42M TOTAL – US$16.84M
INCREASE NET FOREIGN EXCHANGE EARNINGS:	
1.5. Reallocation of resources to provide competitive advantage e.g. moving resources from sugar to more financially viable crops or changing the economics of sugar such as through ethanol – assume five percent benefit per annum from production value increase	Year 1 – US$ 18.44M Year 2 - US$ 18.44M Year 3 – US$ 18.44M Year 4 – US$ 18.44M Year 5 – US$ 18.44M TOTAL – US$ 92.21M
1.6. Fiscal policies such as tax breaks to encourage greater export earnings – assume two percent benefit on total FX earning sector	Year 1 – US$ 43.56M Year 2 - US$ 43.56M Year 3 – US$ 43.56M Year 4 – US$ 43.56M Year 5 – US$ 43.56M TOTAL – US$ 217.82M

1.7. Productivity improvements in FX earnings sectors – assume a ten percent benefit on export earnings value	Year 1 – US$ 217.82M
	Year 2 - US$ 217.82M
	Year 3 – US$ 217.82M
	Year 4 – US$ 217.82M
	Year 5 – US$ 217.82M
	TOTAL – US$1089.10M
1.8. Reduction of GOVERNMENT involvement and bureaucracy in the economy – assume a five percent benefit on total production	Year 2 – US$ 38.52M
	Year 3 – US$ 38.52M
	Year 4 – US$ 38.52M
	Year 5 – US$ 38.52M
	TOTAL – US$154.10M

These fiscal initiatives are examples of what can be done to change the GDP relationship between export and non-export sectors. Some of these initiatives are conservative and can actually accrue a greater benefit as well as some benefits may not accrue immediately. The essence of this example is to try and capture the principle of the long term benefits of fiscal policy over monetary policy.

The benefits of these initiatives can be represented as resulting in the benefits to the net foreign exchange earnings as shown in Table 28.

	Now US$M	Year 1 US$M	Year 2 US$M	Year 3 US$M	Year 4 US$M	Year 5 US$M
Foreign exchange earning sectors						
Agriculture, forestry and fishing	368.83	416.21	506.66	597.10	687.54	777.99
Mining, quarrying and refining	269.10	303.67	343.00	382.33	421.66	460.98
Manufacture	584.78	659.90	745.37	830.83	916.30	1,001.76
Food, beverages and tobacco	324.74	366.46	413.92	461.38	508.84	556.30
Other manufacturing	260.04	293.45	331.45	369.45	407.46	445.46
Hotels and restaurants	370.71	418.33	472.51	526.69	580.87	635.05
	2,178.20	2,458.02	2,812.90	3,167.78	3,522.66	3,877.54
Non foreign exchange earning sectors						
Electricity, gas and wate	230.32	230.32	215.40	200.04	184.77	169.35
Construction	597.70	597.70	558.99	519.12	479.49	439.48
Wholesale & retail trade, Repairs & installation of machinery	1,299.46	1,299.46	1,178.75	1,058.15	940.83	825.78
Transport, storage & communications	846.44	771.10	645.81	599.75	553.97	507.74
Finance & insurance services	768.19	768.19	718.43	667.19	616.26	564.83
Real estate renting & business activities	665.73	665.73	622.60	578.20	534.06	489.49
Producers of government services	801.74	801.74	711.28	660.55	610.12	559.21
Other services	459.43	459.43	429.67	399.03	368.57	337.81
	5,669.01	5,593.67	5,080.93	4,682.03	4,288.07	3,893.69
TOTAL GDP	7,847.21	8,051.69	7,893.83	7,849.81	7,810.73	7,771.23
Surplus/(Deficit)	(3,490.81)	(3,135.65)	(2,268.03)	(1,514.25)	(765.41)	(16.15)
GDP growth		2.6%	-2.0%	-0.6%	-0.5%	-0.5%

Table 28 shows that over the five year period there may not be any economic growth, as the economic structure is reordered. In fact Jamaica could actually see negative economic growth as the policy initiatives and resource reallocation takes effect. Even though there is no economic growth over the period, because resources are limited and are moved from one use to another, the benefits are clear, as the country will increase its net foreign exchange earnings. In this simple example it results in the reduction of the foreign exchange deficit from US$3,491 million to US$17 million. This will no doubt lead to a significant reduction in the need to borrow, and eventually a reduction in the debt, which translates into reduced inflation, and stable interest and exchange rates. As Jamaica improves even more then lower interest and exchange rates would be possible. This simple model illustrates that what Jamaica needs is not economic growth as we have become accustomed to but economic re-engineering, which will result in quality economic growth.

How does this affect Jamaica's currency value?

The question the ordinary man on the street will have is how will this affect Jamaica's currency and ultimately the inflation rate and his individual earnings? After all the real reason for trying to achieve economic development is so that it can make the lives of every Jamaican better, as the United States has successfully done for its citizens over the decades – this implies that the real reason for a government trying to achieve economic development should ultimately be social development.

Let us say that in 2007, when the deficit was US$3.5 billion, the exchange rate was US$1:J$70. The Jamaican dollar would be valued much less than the United States dollar because in 2007 Jamaica demanded much more United States dollars than it earned and so the higher demand for the United States dollar relative to the Jamaican dollar, as importers demanded the United States dollar to facilitate production and meet consumer demand. This means that Jamaicans were willing to pay a higher cost for the United States dollar relative to the Jamaican dollar. Because the demand for Jamaican goods was low then there would not be much demand for its currency.

As Jamaica starts to use less imports, and more local input, and produce more for export - assuming the demand is there - then the demand for Jamaican dollar increases, as the only way to get Jamaican products is to have Jamaican dollars. This demand for Jamaican dollars sends up the price of the Jamaican dollar relative to the United States dollar. The result will be that the Jamaican dollar will revalue against the United States dollar. Thus at the end of Year 5, based on the example, the Jamaican currency would have appreciated significantly against the United States dollar.

This in turn would increase the earnings of the Jamaican worker resulting in an increase in real income levels. There would be a reduced demand for debt, as Jamaica would be earning more than it spends, and fiscal revenues (tax and fees) would increase as there would be increased economic activity and profits. This would translate ultimately into a fiscal surplus, a reduction in the debt/GDP ratio, and more money available for social and infrastructural spending by the government, and ultimately economic development.

Because there is a greater demand for Jamaican products/services, as lower cost production increases and productivity improves, this economic expansion results in expanded Jamaican dollar money supply at lower interest rates. This creates a real expansionary effect on the productive economy.

This illustrates that demand for a country's currency is based on the demand for its products and services globally. So as an example people demand the United States dollar because of the goods and purchases they can purchase in the United States. Importantly also, however, people want to live in the United States because of the quality of life there. **So social development is also an essential ingredient to creating a demand for one's currency**. For example there is a high demand for oil from Iraq, but most people do not want to live in Iraq and so there is not a high demand for Iraq's currency despite the high demand for oil. The argument can therefore be made that the demand for a country's currency has more to do with the quality of life than the products/services it offers, as the latter can more easily be replaced/compromised with products/services from other countries. Jamaica's high crime rate can therefore be seen as a major deterrent to Jamaican dollar appreciation, as a significant reduction could see greater capital inflows into Jamaica.

Bibliography

(n.d.). Retrieved January 2009, from Wikipedia, the online encyclopedia: http://www.wikidpedia.com

Blavy, R. (2006). *Public debt and productivity: The Difficult Quest for growth in Jamaica (IMF Working Paper No WP/06/235).* IMF.

BOJ. (n.d.). *Economic Data.* Retrieved January 2009, from Bank of Jamaica: http://www.boj.org.jm

BOJ. (n.d.). *Publications.* Retrieved January 2009, from Bank of Jamaica: http://www.boj.org.jm

Chung, D. (2008, October 17). Is capitalism dead? *Jamaica Observer* .

Chung, D. (2008, November 7). Yes we can Jamaica. *Jamaica Observer* .

FOOD AND AGRICULTURE ORGANIZATION OF THE UNITED NATIONS. (2003). Retrieved 2009 January, from WTO Agreement on Agriculture: The Implementation Experience - Developing Country Case Studies: http://www.fao.org/docrep/005/y4632e/y4632e00.htm

IMF. (2000). IMF Staff Country Report No 00/19.

IMF. (n.d.). *IMF World Economic Database.* Retrieved January 2009, from International Monetary Fund: http://www.imf.org/external/pubs/

Inter-American Development Bank. (2003). *Jamaica - Productivity and Competitiveness in the Jamaican Economy.*

'Ja lagging in productivity' - Experts say country behind Barbados et al - Wages and labour costs named as factors. (2002, November 18). *Jamaica Gleaner* .

MOFP. (n.d.). *Debt Management.* Retrieved January 2009, from The Ministry of Fiunance and the Public Service.

MOFP. (n.d.). *Fiscal Accounts.* Retrieved January 2009, from The Ministry of Fiunance and the Public Service: http://www.mof.org.jm

MOFP. (2008). *Jamaica Public Bodies Estimates of Revenues and Expenditure for the Year Ending March 2008.*

MOFP. (n.d.). *The Budget*. Retrieved January 2009, from The Ministry of Finance and the Public Service.

PIOJ. (2007). Economic and Social Survey Jamaica 2006.

STATIN. (2007). Demographic Statistics 2006.

STATIN. (2007). *The Labour Force 2006*.

The World Factbook. (2008). Retrieved January 2009, from Central Intelligence Agency: http://www.cia.gov/library/publications/the-world-factbook/index.html

UNCTAD. (2008). *World Investment Report*. Retrieved January 2009, from United Nations Conference on Trade and Development.

UNDP. (2008). Human Development Report 2007/08.

www.ingramcontent.com/pod-product-compliance
Lightning Source LLC
Chambersburg PA
CBHW081129170526
45165CB00008B/2607